# GOD'S SPIRIT
## IN
## WORK AND WORD

# God's Spirit
# in
# Work and Word

## FRED PEARCE

THE CHRISTADELPHIAN
404 SHAFTMOOR LANE
BIRMINGHAM B28 8SZ

1989

*First published 1989*

ISBN 0 85189 126 8

Reproduced from copy supplied.
Printed and bound in Great Britain
by Billing and Sons Limited
Worcester

# PREFACE

THE circumstances which led to the writing of this book have a certain significance for us in our days. Some time ago the author was handed a document in which, it was claimed, Bible teaching about the Spirit was set out. A short perusal soon revealed that the passages quoted were being interpreted in an unsatisfactory manner. They were all from the New Testament and were being put forward as evidence, with little or no attempt to relate them to their immediate context or to the general teaching of the Scriptures about the Spirit of God.

The study of those passages resulted in the series of articles, "The Word and the Spirit" which appeared in *The Christadelphian* Magazine (September 1983—April 1984). The present work is a considerable expansion of that material. Part I shows how God has used the power of His Spirit to promote His authority and the knowledge of His will among His people, first in Israel and then in the communities of believers in Christ.

In Part II significant passages in the New Testament involving "the Spirit" and "the Holy Spirit" are carefully examined. It is hoped that earnest readers of the Scriptures will find in those pages some help to their right understanding.

The author acknowledges his indebtedness to L. G. Sargent's article on "The Spirit of God" in *The Christadelphian*, 1964, pages 293-297; to A. H. Nicholls' book on *The Spirit of God*; and to the Magazine Committee's article on "The Work of the Spirit" in *The Christadelphian*, 1983, pages 297-299, and commends them all to his readers.

No-one can attempt to write on this subject without feeling his inadequacy to express all that God has revealed of Himself, and of His will for His people. Yet "unto us God hath revealed (it) through his Spirit". So we have received "not the spirit which is of the world, but the spirit which is of God". For this every sincere servant of the Lord, humbled by His grace, will not cease to give thanks.

FRED PEARCE

# FOREWORD

"GOD is a Spirit: and they that worship him must worship him in spirit and in truth" (John 4:24). This is what Jesus revealed to the woman by the well of Samaria about his Father, and the satisfactory means of approach to Him that true believers must accept.

To understand something of the mind of God Himself is an outstanding privilege. To be promised some likeness to that mind by a devotion to its expression in written form in the Scriptures of truth is a promise almost beyond belief. Yet it is this great theme of how God works, and of how He is a God of purpose and order who wishes that men and women will serve Him, that is explored in this carefully researched book. There should be no surprise that the conclusions reached in it direct thinking men and women to the Bible as the only complete revelation of the plan of salvation available. God's Word becomes His work. Did not the Word become flesh in the Lord Jesus Christ? And did not numberless events occur "according to the word of the Lord"?

This vital subject, and this work in its attempt to expound it, are thus recommended to the careful attention of the reader. As he turns refreshed to the Scriptures may he "grow in grace, and in the knowledge of our Lord and Saviour" (2 Peter 3:18).

MICHAEL ASHTON

# CONTENTS

Preface .................................................. v

Foreword ............................................... vi

PART I

1. Introduction ....................................... 1

2. Through the Law and the Prophets .......... 3

3. In the Days of Jesus and the Apostles ...... 20

4. The Spirit and the Word ................... 36

5. "The Spirit" in the English Text .......... 50

6. "The Mind of the Spirit" ................. 54

PART II

7. Various Passages Considered .............. 60

8. "Spirit" and "Holy Spirit" ............... 81

9. The Abiding ........................... 108

10. Conclusions........................... 119

Appendix .................................... 125

Index of Principal Passages Discussed ........... 127

# Part I

# 1

## INTRODUCTION

*"But ye are not in the flesh, but in the spirit, if so be that the Spirit of God dwell in you. Now if any man have not the Spirit of Christ, he is none of his."* (Romans 8:9)

THESE striking words of the Apostle Paul reveal to us how important it is that we should clearly understand "the Spirit of God" and "the Spirit of Christ". In fact he is clearly asserting that if we do not manifest in the right way "the Spirit of Christ", we can make no claim to being a member of his people. But how can we "have" the Spirit of Christ, if we do not understand what it is, or indeed if our ideas about it are quite wrong?

The subject has become all the more urgent for all those who would be Christ's true followers, by the babble of voices in the modern religious world, all claiming to recognise "the Spirit", whether it be by "gifts" such as tongues or healings, by the emotional response aroused by hymn singing, or by any other method. The "charismatic" movement has had a profound effect upon the membership of all religious communities: Catholics, Anglicans, Methodists and Baptists have all been affected, and so have smaller communities. It has had the effect of dividing its members into two camps—those who adopt the "charismatic" procedures, and those who reject them. But it has also united members from differing communities who have been willing to abandon some of their old religious convictions in favour of a common, largely emotional expression of their faith.

1

Inevitably, in such a situation the members of any religious community will come under the modern influence. Young people especially encounter it in schools and colleges and find it appealing. By "the Spirit of Christ" most religious people understand chiefly his mercy, compassion and forgiveness towards all. Yet is this what the Apostle Paul had in mind when he said we must not be "in the flesh" but "in the spirit" if we are to share "the Spirit of God", and "the Spirit of Christ"?

## Where to Find the Truth?

How shall we find the answer to such an important question as this? One fact should weigh heavily with us. How do we know anything at all about God or Christ anyway? The answer is clear: because the Bible tells us in great detail. It is our only source. We have nowhere else to go, except to the pronouncements of some human mind or group of human minds, no matter who they are or what claims they make for themselves. It is to the Word of God itself that we must go for the vital understanding we need. Happily we have it easily available—the very same writings of the Law, the Psalms and the Prophets (the Old Testament) which were accepted and used by Jesus himself, and his apostles after him; the very writings of those apostles (the New Testament) to believers in those early times. No authority has arisen since able to supersede what was "written for our learning". It has been well said that if what Jesus and his apostles taught in the first century was truth, then it is truth still. That is "the truth" we need for our understanding in these confused days. How blessed we are to have it so easily available!

The Scriptures reveal to us how, ever since the Creation, God has been active in human affairs. In the following pages we shall examine how He has manifested His Spirit at various times to achieve His purpose of "taking out of the nations a people for his name". This will require a rapid survey of events in the lives of God's people, in order to provide a general understanding of His method and aim. In Part II of this book there is undertaken a careful examination of many passages in the New Testament concerning the Spirit, with the aim of making clear just what the inspired writers meant by their use of the term. It is, after all, *their* understanding which is vital to us.

2

# 2

# THROUGH THE LAW AND
# THE PROPHETS

IT is easy to make a serious mistake at the beginning of our
quest by imagining that "the Spirit" must have a great deal
to do with Christ and the early believers, and therefore it is to the
New Testament alone we need go. But this is to ignore the
fundamental truth that the Spirit has to do with *God*, for we shall
find that it is the expression of Himself, in all His activities. Now
the Bible's revelation of God begins long before New Testament
times. It is to the Old Testament, then, that we must turn for a
sound basic understanding. In any case Jesus and his apostles
constantly referred to the writings of the Law and the Prophets.
It ought not to surprise us to discover that there is a marvellous
harmony in the way the Spirit of God is presented in both Old
and New Testaments.

## The Spirit

The word 'spirit' in the Old Testament is a good example of the
way a Hebrew term begins with a basic idea, then expands into
a number of closely related senses. *Ruach*, derived from a verb
meaning to blow or to breathe, conveys the idea of air in motion.
So it is 90 times translated 'wind':

> *"God made a **wind** to pass over the earth."*      (Genesis 8:1)

When the air is in the nostrils of a man, then it means breath (28
times), and so naturally the life which results from breathing:

> *"I do bring a flood of waters upon the earth, to destroy all flesh,
> wherein is the **breath** of life."*      (Genesis 6:17)

Then the word is used of the *mental* life, the mind of an individual. Esau's action in taking two Hittite women as wives was:

*"a grief of **mind** unto Isaac and to Rebekah"* (Genesis 26:35, where the margin tells us the original is *a bitterness of spirit*).

Rahab, describing the effects upon the inhabitants of Jericho of the news of God's mighty works in Egypt, says:

> *"As soon as we had heard these things, our hearts did melt, neither did there remain any more **courage** (R.V. spirit) in any man."*
>
> (Joshua 2:11)

The psalmist uses 'spirit' to describe the attitude of mind of the true servants of God:

> *"Blessed is the man unto whom the Lord imputeth not iniquity, and in whose **spirit** there is no guile."* (Psalm 32:2)

> *"The Lord . . . saveth such as be of a contrite **spirit**."*
>
> (Psalm 34:18)

Our brief survey of typical passages shows that 'spirit' conveys not just the life of the body, but much more significantly the *life of the mind*. We shall find this principle of great importance in our study.

## The Spirit and Power of God

We find no difficulty in appreciating that the 'physical' nature of God is vastly different from our own "flesh and blood". The Apostle Paul sums it up thus:

> *"Now unto the King **eternal, incorruptible,** invisible, the only God, be honour and glory for ever and ever. Amen."*
>
> (1 Timothy 1:17, R.V.)

> *". . . the blessed and only Potentate (Sovereign, R.S.V.), the King of kings, and Lord of lords; who only hath **immortality,** dwelling in light unapproachable; whom no man hath seen nor can see: to whom be honour and power eternal. Amen."*
>
> (1 Timothy 6:15-16, R.V.)

The same apostle declares that the nations in their ignorance

> *"became vain in their imaginations, and their foolish heart was darkened . . . they changed the glory of **the uncorruptible** God into an image made like to corruptible man."*
>
> (Romans 1:21-23)

4

The contrast with the nature of man is expressed thus by Isaiah:

> *"Now the Egyptians are men, and not God; and their horses flesh, and not spirit . . ."* (31:3)

Here we have two contrasting 'natures': men and flesh on the one hand, and God and spirit on the other.

The idea of God as incorruptible and immortal, by contrast with corruptible and hence mortal human flesh, causes no problem. His nature is Spirit, and not flesh.

The first and most obvious manifestation of this Divine Spirit nature is in *power*. The Lord God created the heavens and the earth:

> *"By his spirit the heavens are garnished . . . these are but the outskirts of his ways . . . the thunder of his power who can understand?"*
> (Job 26:13-14, R.V.)

In delivering His people Israel from the slavery of Egypt, He causes His power to be seen and felt. Looking back over 40 years, Moses could say:

> *"Ask now of the days that are past . . . since the day that God created man upon the earth . . . whether there hath been any such thing as this great thing is . . .? Did ever people hear the voice of God speaking out of the midst of the fire, as thou hast heard, and live? Or hath God assayed to go and take him a nation from the midst of another nation, by trials (R.V.m.), by signs, and by wonders, and by war, and by a mighty hand . . . and by great terrors, according to all that the LORD your God did for you in Egypt before your eyes?"*
> (Deuteronomy 4:32-34)

This is a remarkable factual tribute to the literal deliverance of the nation of Israel from the power of Egypt. It is also a witness to the omnipotence of God: He can achieve any end He desires, by His supreme power if necessary. The same Spirit power was shown from time to time in acts of judgement upon presumptuous men, as when consuming fire descended upon Nadab and Abihu, and the earth opened to swallow the rebellious company of Korah, Dathan and Abiram. This aspect of the Spirit of God is easy to understand. We shall need to return later on to some of its activity.

5

## Why this Demonstration of Power?

But there are important questions to be asked about it, especially about the events of the Exodus. Why was it necessary for God to act with power? There are three significant answers:

1. To bring merited judgements upon the religious system of Egypt, the most highly organised pagan religion of ancient times: their gods (and especially Pharaoh) had to be discredited and the God of Israel be recognised as supreme among the nations:

> *"I will at this time send all my plagues upon thine (Pharaoh's) heart, and upon thy servants, and upon thy people; that thou mayest know that there is* **none like me in all the earth** *... that my name might be declared throughout all the earth."* (Exodus 9:14-16)

How effectively this aim was achieved is shown by two remarkable witnesses. First Rahab, receiving the spies in Jericho:

> *"I know that the LORD hath given you the land, and that your terror is fallen upon us, and that all the inhabitants of the land melt away* (R.V.) *because of you. For* **we have heard** *how the LORD dried up the water of the Red Sea for you, when ye came out of Egypt; and what ye did unto the two kings of the Amorites ... whom ye utterly destroyed. And as soon as we had heard these things,* **our hearts did melt**, *neither did there remain any more courage (spirit, R.V.) in any man, because of you: for the* **LORD your God, he is God** *in heaven above, and in earth beneath."* (Joshua 2:9-11)

This is an outstanding passage. It demonstrates the great effect upon the surrounding nations of the manifestations of Divine power at the Exodus. But an equally striking witness appears long afterwards, when the Philistines hear that the ark of God has been brought into the midst of the army of Israel:

> *"The Philistines were afraid, for they said ... Woe unto us! ... who shall deliver us out of the hand of these mighty Gods (elohim)? These are the Gods that smote the Egyptians with all the plagues in the wilderness."* (1 Samuel 4:7-8)

We need to remind ourselves that this was said about 350 years *after* the events of the Exodus! What a remarkable witness to the tremendous effect those events had upon the minds of the surrounding peoples. That is just what the God of Israel designed them to do. Incidentally, there will be a remarkable modern parallel when the great invading host of Gog is destroyed upon the mountains of Israel, not by any nation's atomic bombs, but by Divine power. As God Himself declares through Ezekiel:

> *"I will be known in the eyes of many nations; and they shall know that I am the LORD . . . I will set my glory among the heathen, and all the heathen shall see my judgment that I have executed, and my hand that I have laid upon them."*     (Ezekiel 38:23; 39:21)

The awe produced by this revelation of God's supremacy will provide the basis for the summons Christ will issue to the whole earth:

> *"Fear God, and give glory to him . . . "*     (Revelation 14:7)

2. The second part of God's purpose was to convince the nation of Israel that God, He who had revealed Himself to their fathers Abraham, Isaac and Jacob with promises, the same who had now spoken to them through His servant Moses, was indeed *their* God; and not only that, but that He was the only One: there was no other. It was "the Lord your God" who did these great things "before your eyes". So, says Moses:

> *"Know therefore this day, and consider it in thine heart, that the LORD he is God in heaven above, and upon the earth beneath: **there is none else.**"*     (Deuteronomy 4:39)

We have some difficulty in appreciating the unique position of Israel in the world of "many gods" in which they lived. All nations had their own gods, and adopted a more or less tolerant attitude towards the gods of others. Amid this universal polytheism there arose a tiny nation who had the amazing arrogance to assert that *their* God, the God of Israel, was the only one who existed, and the gods of all the nations were nothing but pieces of "wood and stone". Nothing was more calculated to provoke the bitter hostility of the surrounding worshippers of pagan gods. Apart from the striking demonstrations of power accompanying Israel's Exodus, no great effect would have been achieved. That remark applies to Israel too. Apart from the clear and effective evidence of the power and favour of their God, the appeal for their faith in Him would have had no convincing basis.

3. But for Israel themselves, there was a development of this. Moses put it briefly thus:

7

*"Out of heaven he made thee to hear his voice,* **that he might instruct thee***: and upon earth he shewed thee his great fire; and* **thou heardest his words** *out of the midst of the fire . . ."*

(Deuteronomy 4:36)

The implication is clear: the purpose of the manifestation of Divine power, both at the Exodus and upon Mount Sinai, was not just to frighten them into submission, though that stage needed to be experienced. "All the people in the camp trembled", we are told, as they witnessed the lightnings and the thick cloud, and heard the thunders and the great voice. The people needed to have a sense of awe and reverence, in order that they might be ready to be "instructed". For human minds true instruction must proceed from authority, for men who do not recognise any authority but their own, are never willing to learn.

*"The meek will (God) teach his way."* (Psalm 25:9)

The others have always been too proud to learn.

We have arrived now at a very important conclusion: the purpose of the exercise of the Spirit of God in power was to produce a situation in which His people could be "instructed". Here is the true work of the Spirit of God, who makes known to His people His words, His thoughts, and the understanding of His ways. We shall find abundant evidence of this as we proceed.

### Moses and Israel's Judges

The next step in the use of God's Spirit as power was to establish, in a way that could not be questioned, the authority of those who were to act on His behalf in what they did and said.

The first great example is Moses, chosen by God Himself, and given authority in the eyes of Israel by the signs which he was empowered to produce. He led the people in the long contention with Pharaoh, demonstrating his divine authority by the fact that the plagues he foretold came to pass, and were removed just as swiftly at his word. In Moses resided the power of God, and Aaron was his "prophet", or spokesman. After the final and spectacular deliverance from Egyptian power at the Red Sea, the effect upon Israel is stated thus:

*"Israel saw the great work which the LORD did upon the Egyptians, and the people feared the LORD: and they believed in the LORD, and in his servant Moses."*                    (Exodus 14:31, R.V.)

So Moses was in a position to go up into the mountain, and to return to his people, bearing with him the commandments of God for them. The Law was given to Israel in circumstances which emphasised the power of their God and the authority of Moses to be a mediator for them. It was in these circumstances that the reputation of the law was established, not just among the leaders, but among the whole community of Israel. Striking events such as those of the Exodus were a sheer necessity if the whole nation was to be impressed with the power of their God and the authority of His chief spokesman. It was an authority which lasted all through Israel's history.

But Moses was not to be alone in his vital work of leadership. The time came when "the burden was too great" for him alone; he could not possibly deal with all the cases which came before him for decision. So God consented in the appointment of seventy others to assist him. Moses chose the seventy according to their spiritual qualifications: "wise men and understanding", "able men, such as fear God, men of truth (that is, faithful to the revelation God had given them through Moses), hating covetousness" (Deuteronomy 1:13; Exodus 18:21). When the seventy were gathered together:

*"The LORD came down in a cloud ... and took of the spirit that was upon him (Moses), and gave it unto the seventy elders: and it came to pass, that, when the spirit rested upon them, they prophesied ... "*                    (Numbers 11:25)

In other words they broke into spontaneous praise of God, glorifying His name.

Here there occurs a remarkable change in the versions, for where the A.V. concludes: "they prophesied, and did not cease", the R.V., R.S.V. and modern versions all agree that the sense should be rather the opposite: "they did *so no more.*"

There are significant conclusions to be drawn from this episode. First, these men are not chosen by the people, but by Moses (no democratic principle here!). They were chosen upon two grounds: their standing as elders among the people, and their

9

qualifications of mind (wisdom, truth, faithfulness, not self-seeking) were such as Moses had himself. In other words they shared his spirit, his attitude of mind—this was their great qualification. But it was a necessary basis of their authority as judges for the whole people that they should be seen to have the approval of God. This God provided by the direct Spirit gift which caused them to prophesy, evidently in a group and simultaneously. But the direct Spirit gift *ceased* after a time and they prophesied in that way no more.

An important principle arises from this interesting case: where God has granted special powers to men who act on His behalf, it has been with the direct purpose, first of glorifying God, and then of adding the divine authority to *the words* His servants spoke, the message they delivered. It was not the miraculous gift which was the most important thing: it was the word of God which was to be uttered. The Spirit gift was the means of giving powerful support to that word.

## The Significance of Elijah and Elisha

Other works of God in power, recorded in the Old Testament, have the same aims. The remarkable cases of Elijah and Elisha are an interesting example. They were prophets performing mighty works, but they left no written record of their prophetic sayings, as did Isaiah, Jeremiah, Ezekiel and the rest. Why was this unusual and varied demonstration of Divine power granted through Elijah and Elisha, but not through their prophetic successors?

The key to the answer is in the fact that their ministry was to the Northern Kingdom, Israel, at a time of great apostasy. Under the influence of faithless kings and an idolatrous queen, Jezebel, the worship of the Canaanite 'baalim' (gods of fertility) had spread widely among the Israelites. The priests of Baal were honoured by the rulers of the kingdom and were to be numbered in hundreds. The abandonment of the true worship of the God of Israel and of His Law was so widespread that even Elijah was constrained to say, "I, even I only, am left". Amid such widespread disaffection, the word of a prophet would have had only a limited effect. So the God of heaven granted the prayer of His servant Elijah:

*"LORD God of Abraham, Isaac, and of Israel, let it be known this day that thou art God in Israel, and that I am thy servant, and that I have done all these things at thy word."* (1 Kings 18:36)

By contrast with the powerlessness of Baal and his worshippers, fire descended upon Carmel and consumed the water-drenched burnt offering, and the fickle people fell on their faces exclaiming, "The Lord, he is the God".

Their conversion was short-lived. But a striking witness had been given to the whole nation of the unique supremacy of the God of Israel, and their rejection of the clear lesson of Carmel was the basis for their ultimate judgement as a people. However, there *were* still a few faithful in Israel: God Himself declared to Elijah that there were 7,000 men. Their hearts would be strengthened, other waverers would no doubt be encouraged, and those of alert mind in Judah must surely have been impressed by the great sign of God's supremacy which had taken place. Once again the purpose of the display of Divine miraculous power was to confirm the faith of those who were still capable of understanding.

## God's Spiritual Purpose

But the purpose of God with His people Israel was not only to impress them with the sense of His uniqueness and supremacy, but—as we have seen—to "instruct them". The greatest basic "instruction" was the portrait of Himself, in all His spiritual and moral character, as a great contrast to the gods of the surrounding nations.

In Isaiah we find a most helpful starting point. In chapter 63 the prophet describes the attitude God had shown towards His wayward people:

*"I will mention the **lovingkindnesses** of the LORD ... and the great **goodness** toward the house of Israel, which he hath bestowed on them according to his **mercies**, and according to the multitude of his **lovingkindnesses**. For he said, Surely they are my people ... so he was their **Saviour**. In all their affliction he was **afflicted** ... in his **love** and his **pity** he redeemed them."* (verses 7-9)

This is not a portrait of a neutral, colourless God, indifferent to His people. It is the picture of a real personality, vitally concerned over their true welfare. Now Isaiah adds this:

*"But they rebelled, and **grieved his holy spirit**."*

(verse 10, R.V.)

Now what does "holy spirit" mean here? Evidently it cannot be a reference to God's miraculous power—it was not *that* which was grieved. Two parallel references in the Psalms will enlighten us:

*"How oft did they (Israel) provoke him in the wilderness, and **grieve** him in the desert!"* (78:40)

*"Forty years long was I **grieved** with that generation."*

(95:10, R.V.)

So to grieve God's Holy Spirit was to grieve *Him* as a personality, in His divine consciousness, in His very character. The Apostle Paul exhorts the Ephesians in the same way: "Grieve not the holy Spirit of God" (4:30) by conduct inconsistent with His high and holy calling.

Where shall we find our best description of this 'holy spirit' of God which is the essence of His character? Where better than in God's own description of Himself? Moses desired to be shown God's "glory". God replied:

*"I will make all my **goodness** pass before thee, and I will proclaim the **name** of the LORD before thee ... "* (Exodus 33:19)

*"The LORD ... proclaimed, The LORD, the LORD, a God full of compassion and gracious, slow to anger and plenteous in mercy and truth; keeping mercy for thousands, forgiving iniquity and transgression and sin: and that will by no means clear the guilty."*

(Exodus 34:6-7, R.V.)

Here is the Spirit of God, in His great mercy and forgiveness, and yet His utter holiness which will not allow Him to tolerate sin for ever. It is that combination of grace and truth which Moses calls "the power of the Lord" (Numbers 14:17-19). Paul describes it as "the goodness and severity of God" (Romans 11:22). This is the significance of the "Name of the Lord". It describes His moral and spiritual character, which is constantly proclaimed by His prophets (see, for instance, Psalm 103:7-9).

### The Spirit and the Messiah

One of the most helpful passages upon this aspect of the spirit of the LORD is found in Isaiah's prophecy of the coming Son of David:

12

*"The spirit of the LORD shall rest upon him, the spirit of wisdom and understanding, the spirit of counsel and might, the spirit of knowledge and of the fear of the LORD; and shall make him of quick understanding in the fear of the LORD . . . with righteousness shall he judge the poor, and reprove with equity for the meek of the earth."*

(11:2-4)

Wisdom, understanding, counsel, knowledge, the fear of the LORD, righteousness, equity—these are to be the effects of the spirit of the LORD on the Messiah to come. Clearly they are all *qualities of mind* and character. It is unlikely that "might" even, in the midst of these spiritual qualities, is any reference to the miraculous powers he was to possess. It is rather that strength of character of one who is wholly devoted to the service of God. We shall find the same "might" in the case of John the Baptist among others.

The conclusion so far is clear and very important. The Spirit of God, sometimes called the Holy Spirit, has two aspects: first, the incorruptible and eternal nature of God, and the supreme powers which flow from it, in His control of the natural world, for the advancement of His will. Second, the sheer quality of the Divine mind, expressed in God's thoughts and purposes, and in all His communications with mankind. The first is a natural power which enables Him to achieve His ends, despite human resistance; the second is a moral power, capable of influencing those members of the human race "who are of good and honest hearts" (Luke 8:15). An understanding of these two aspects of the Spirit of God will be of vital importance when we come to examine some of the sayings of the New Testament.

## The Spiritual Purpose of the Law

The purpose of God with His people Israel was to train them in an understanding of His own spiritual character, so that they might become fit subjects for His kingdom, reflecting His glory in their own ways. So the aim of the Law was not punitive, but educative. The Israelites were required to perceive the spiritual meaning of all God conveyed to them for their observance. The discerning Israelite should hence have seen in circumcision the need to curb the natural desires of the flesh. As Moses put it to them, "Circumcise therefore the foreskin of your heart"

13

Deuteronomy 10:16), showing how well he had grasped the meaning. The Israelite's keeping of the sabbath was to be no mere mechanical observance, for he was to keep it *"unto* the LORD" (5:14, R.V.), and was to remember on that day how God had delivered him from the slavery of Egypt—in other words, the great mercy God had shown him in his own redemption. When the worshipper came to the door of the tabernacle with his offering, he was to lay his hand upon the head of the victim and to be reminded that it was dying on his behalf, "to make atonement for him" (Leviticus 1:4). When he was commanded to act in mercy towards the poor, the fatherless and the widows in his community, it was because he was remembering that God had delivered *him* in mercy from the hopeless bondage of Egypt: so he must show a similar mercy towards others:

> *"Thou shalt remember that thou wast a bondman in Egypt, and the LORD thy God redeemed thee thence:* **therefore** *I command thee to do this thing."* (Deuteronomy 24:18)

So with all the requirements of the Law. They were intended to have an influence upon the understanding of the Israelites, and to promote the growth of their understanding of the wisdom of God. This was to be the effect of the revelation to them of the spiritual character of God, and of His wise laws for the ordering of their lives. What He desired was not a people mechanically carrying out the letter of His Law, but one which had absorbed the Spirit of His mind, and was therefore fit to be called His "son". For, as He said through Hosea,

> *"I desired mercy, and not sacrifice; and the knowledge of God more than burnt offerings."* (Hosea 6:6)

Here is the spiritual purpose of the Law. The true sense of this saying may be expressed thus: "I desired not so much sacrifice as mercy, and not so much burnt offerings as the knowledge of God." The sacrifices had to be made, but they should have been offered with spiritual understanding.

The witness of the New Testament to the spiritual influence of the law is decisive. Jesus declared that the scribes and Pharisees were tithing "mint and anise and cummin" (that is, they were pernickety about mere details of observance), but they had "omitted (left undone, R.V.) the weightier matters of the law, judgment, mercy, and faith'' (Matthew 23:23). It is easy to imagine the incredulity of the Jews on being told that mercy and faith were ''more weighty'' than circumcision and the keeping of the sabbath! But Jesus' saying shows clearly what God's real purpose was. So the Apostle Paul describes the commandments of the law as ''holy, and just, and good'', and adds that ''the law is spiritual'' (Romans 7:12,14): that is to say, its aim was to influence the mind, or spirit of God's people. Referring to Gentiles who knew not the Law but had come to know and believe the gospel, he says they ''shew *the work of the law* written in their hearts'' (Romans 2:15)—a revealing phrase which shows that the Law was designed to produce a certain effect upon the minds of those who observed it: a ''spiritual'' effect.

This was the work of the Spirit of God through the Law of Moses.

**How was it achieved?**
At first, by the direct commands of God to Israel, delivered through Moses ''face to face''. But immediately there is a development:

> *''Moses ... told the people all the words of the LORD, and all the judgements: and all the people answered with one voice and said, All the words which the LORD hath spoken will we do.* **And Moses wrote all the words of the LORD** *...''* (Exodus 24:3-4)

> *''***Moses wrote this law,*** and delivered it unto the priests ... And Moses commanded them, saying, At the end of every seven years ... in the feast of tabernacles, when all Israel is come to appear before the LORD ...* **thou shalt read this law** *before all Israel in their hearing. Gather the people together, men, women, and children ... that they may* **hear,** *and ...* **learn,** *and* **fear** *the LORD your God, and observe to do all the words of this law: and that their children, which have not known any thing, may hear, and learn to fear the LORD your God.''* (Deuteronomy 31:9-13)

Here we have a most important and significant principle: the authentic Word of God is now no longer to be expected through the direct voice of God or through His angels. It is written down, for all to hear and read. The written record is the authoritative voice of God for Israel, and it must be read and received as such. In fact, by Divine command a copy is to be put by the side of the ark of the covenant, "that it may be there *for a witness against thee;* for I know thy rebellion and stiff neck . . ." In times of apostasy the true voice of God would be found in the written record Moses had made at His command. When Israel would in later times set up a king over themselves,

> *"he shall write him a copy of this law in a book out of that which is before the priests . . . and it shall be with him, and he shall* **read therein all the days of his life***: that he may learn to fear the LORD his God, to keep all the words of this law . . . that his heart be not lifted up above his brethren . . . "* (Deuteronomy 17:18-20)

When Moses has been laid to rest, Joshua succeeded to the onerous task of leading the people. Where was Joshua to find the guidance and wisdom he needed? From some continuing oral revelation of God? From his own knowledge of Moses' ways? Not at all. This is what he was told by the Lord:

> *"Be thou strong and very courageous, that thou mayest observe to do according to all the law, which Moses my servant commanded thee: turn not from it to the right hand or to the left . . .* **This book of the law shall not depart out of thy mouth***; but thou shalt meditate therein day and night, that thou mayest observe to do according to all that is written therein."* (Joshua 1:7-8)

This, then, is the way God deliberately chose to carry on His spiritual work with Israel. It is to be noted that the existence and authority of the written record in Israel was not a matter of human tradition. It was explicitly established by Divine command. It was God's own chosen method of preserving and propagating the knowledge of Himself, of His Spirit. But the implications of this are tremendous. This written Word of God must be capable of conveying the very mind of God; it is the vehicle of His Spirit. And how does it do this? By conveying truth and the knowledge of God in a way that can be *understood*. It is not primarily an appeal to human emotion, but to the reasonable comprehension of sincere minds, willing to be taught in Divine ways and desiring to absorb the Spirit of God's mind by their humble submission to His will. This is what the Apostle must have meant when he wrote to the Romans that the life of submission to the Lord was their "reasonable service" *(logikēn latreian)* (Romans 12:2). The word of God is not irrational, erratic, or inconsistent. It is a true expression of the wisdom, or Spirit, of God. As the writer of Proverbs expresses it,

> *"Wisdom ... uttereth her voice in the streets ... Turn you at my reproof: behold, I will pour out **my spirit** unto you, I will make known **my words** unto you."*                (Proverbs 1:20-23)

So the spirit of the wisdom of God is expressed in His words. No wonder the written word of God had such a reputation for spiritual power among the faithful in Israel. Consider David's testimony:

> *"The law of the LORD is perfect, **restoring the soul**: the testimony of the LORD is sure, **making wise** the simple. The precepts of the LORD are right, **rejoicing the heart**: the commandment of the LORD is pure, **enlightening the eyes** ... The judgements of the LORD are true and righteous altogether ... Moreover by them is thy servant **warned** ..."*                (Psalm 19:7-11, R.V.)

It is the Apostle Paul who tells us clearly how this power of the word arises: "All scripture is given by inspiration of God"— literally "is God-breathed" (2 Timothy 3:16). The breath or spirit of God is in them all. That is why they can "restore the soul", "make wise", "enlighten" and "warn". But more of this when we come to consider New Testament times.

## The Prophets

The prophets (apart from Elijah and Elisha who left no writings) performed hardly any miraculous signs. The work of the Spirit of God was carried on in their days through the words they spoke, always "the word of the Lord". Their message was no new doctrine, but a recall to the original revelation given by God through Moses. The emphasis of their message is consistently the same: it is to recognise their God who had delivered them out of the land of Egypt, to worship Him, to obey His commandments, and to manifest that spirit of mercy and truth which His service required. In other words, it was a call to "know" their God through the revelation He had made to them. As Proverbs again has it:

> *"The fear of the LORD is the beginning of wisdom: and the **knowledge of the Holy One** is understanding."*
>                (Proverbs 9:10, R.V.)

It was this "knowledge of God", the understanding of His Spirit and His ways, which the words of the prophets were designed to achieve. In time, their words were written down and were added to "the law" and "the psalms" to form the whole body of written revelation in Old Testament times. In the years of faithlessness, idolatry and corruption, the devout men and women of Israel found that instruction in God's will, that guidance for their lives, and that stimulus to faith which enabled them to "wait upon the Lord". They were the humble and contrite spirits, honouring the Word of God, whom He looked upon with favour. Among them the work of the Spirit of God proceeded through His Word which they possessed. To reverent and earnest minds it conveyed all that they needed for their life of humble faith.

Thus was the basis laid in Old Testament times for the preparation of a people for the Name of the Lord. We shall find that our understanding of this will be of great assistance when we come to consider the work of the Spirit in the age of the gospel.

### Between the Testaments

After the witness of Haggai, Zechariah and Malachi (the last of the prophets) to the exiles who had returned to Jerusalem from Babylon, there followed 400 years of darkness. During these four long centuries, until John the Baptist appeared in Israel, there was, as far as we know, no prophet in Israel speaking "the word of the Lord", no open interventions by God or His angels. It does not take much imagination to realise the severe trial of faith which this imposed upon the earnest worshippers of the God of Israel. The remnant of the nation suffered invasions of foreign powers and desecration of the temple. Even the remarkable resurgence of Israelite power under the Maccabees ended in the tyranny of Rome. How the faithful must have agonised over the fate of Israel. "Lord, what has happened to the promises to our fathers? Where is the promised Son of David? Lord, how long . . .?"

Had the work of the Spirit of God ceased among Israel during these dark centuries? Not at all. The faithful did what they have always done: having no direct message from God, they turned to the written records—to the Law, the Prophets, and the Psalms. In them they found that assurance for their faith, that instruction in the worship and the service of God, and that guidance for the spirit of their lives. "They that feared the LORD spake often one to another", no doubt around the revered scrolls which were the Word of God for them. So the work of the Spirit of God went on freely among those who were willing to read, to believe, and to obey.

But they had one explicit encouragement in their age. The eleventh chapter of Daniel's prophecy contained a remarkable forecast of the comings and goings of the "king of the north" and the "king of the south" through the land of Israel. The campaigns and intrigues of the kings of Syria and Egypt, the Seleucids and the Ptolemies, were prophesied in remarkable detail so that discerning Israelites would have been able to see the actual fulfilment in their own days. The eleventh chapter of Daniel was a 'miniature Apocalypse' for the waiting saints of those days. It was the assurance that the purpose of God was proceeding and that the promised end would come.

Have we not here a remarkable parallel in our own case? We too live in an age of darkness, with no direct revelations from God. We too have "the word of God", the holy Scriptures, "God-breathed", able to make us wise unto salvation. We too have the encouragement of the book of Revelation, with its prophetic evidence of the purpose of God in history. For us too the work of the Spirit goes on, as the Word of God is read, understood, and believed, and the minds of faithful men and women are "renewed" and recreated after the pattern of the Spirit of God.

# 3

# IN THE DAYS OF JESUS AND
# THE APOSTLES

A S the days of darkness drew to their close, and the time of
the prophesied manifestation of "Messiah the Prince"
(Daniel 9:25) approached, a new era opened in God's dealings
with His people. It was significant for a series of Divine interventions in the life of Israel, all manifestations of His Spirit as power,
but not all seen as such at first.

## John the Baptist

The *first* intervention occurred in the person of John the Baptist.
He was a son promised in their old age to a faithful pair,
Zacharias and Elizabeth. An angel appeared to Zacharias as he
was ministering in the temple, and predicted the birth of John:

> *". . . he shall be great in the sight of the Lord . . . and he shall be
> filled with the Holy Spirit, even from his mother's womb. And many
> of the children of Israel shall he turn to the Lord their God. And he
> (John) shall go before him (God)* **in the spirit and power of
> Elias (Elijah)** *. . . "*                      (Luke 1:15-17)

Now this is a remarkable saying, for Elijah was known for his
miraculous powers in his witness for the God of Israel; but John
the Baptist was not. In fact, it was said of him, "John *did no
miracle*" (John 10:41). How then did John share the "spirit and
power of Elijah"? There is only one solution: the power of John
the Baptist was not miraculous, it was spiritual. The prophecy
evidently meant "in the *spiritual power* of Elijah", that is in his
utter devotion to the service of the Lord and the strength of his
conviction and faith; in his resolve to pursue his call to repentance, and his warnings of divine judgement, even to a nation

20

whose leaders rejected him. So Luke described John's early years: "the child grew, and *waxed strong in spirit* ..." (1:80).

Thus the intervention of God in the raising up of John the Baptist produced, not a miracle-working prophet, but one filled with zeal for His honour and service. His message was the verdict of the Spirit of God upon rebellious Israel. Micah had expressed the same 700 years earlier:

> *"But truly I am full of power, even* (R.V.m) *the spirit of the Lord, and of judgement, and of might, to declare unto Jacob his transgression, and to Israel his sin."* (Micah 3:8)

Micah, too, "did no miracle", but his message was one of power and truth because it was the expression of "the Spirit of the Lord". In this way, John the Baptist was truly in the line of the prophets of Israel. The work of the Spirit through him was carried out by the truth and the power of the message he proclaimed.

### The Birth of Jesus

The *second* intervention was at first known to very few. It was that direct action of the Holy Spirit by which Jesus was born of Mary. About this the Gospel of Luke is clear and precise. The birth of Jesus took place because the Holy Spirit "came upon" Mary and the power of the Highest "overshadowed" her. This was a work of the Spirit which only the Almighty Himself could achieve, in order that the child born should be, in the fullest sense, Son of God. However, as we shall see, the purpose of this divine intervention was to make it possible for the Son to manifest "the Spirit" of his Father, in all His "grace and truth". Once more a miraculous act was intended to have a "spiritual" result. The Son became the manifestation of the character and mind of God.

### The Powers of Jesus

The *third* intervention was in the equipment of Jesus with the necessary powers for the preaching of the gospel and the preparation of a community of believers.

The aim was to provide a witness to the whole nation, as a continuation of the message of John. It was first a call to repentance: in fact, according to Matthew's Gospel, Jesus opened his ministry by saying: "Repent". Then he added: "for the kingdom of heaven is at hand" (Matthew 4:17).

21

But Jesus emerged in Israel from the despised province of Galilee, notorious for its numerous Gentiles. Also he seemed to have no distinguished antecedents. How could "this man" be the illustrious Son of David? So God granted him special powers to give him authority in Israel, so that his preaching might receive greater attention. At his baptism by John, and his transfiguration on the mount, there were special manifestations of the power of the Spirit, with the same basic message: "This is my beloved Son; hear ye him". But the most striking and effective aid granted to him was his power to heal. Here is Matthew's testimony to the effect of Jesus' activities in the early days of his preaching:

> *"Jesus went about in all Galilee, teaching in their synagogues, and preaching the gospel of the kingdom, and healing all manner of disease and . . . of sickness among the people. And the report of him went forth into all Syria: and they brought unto him all that were sick, holden with divers diseases and torments, possessed with devils . . . epileptic, and palsied; and he healed them. And there followed him great multitudes of people from Galilee, and Decapolis, and Jerusalem, and Judaea, and from beyond Jordan"* (Matthew 4:23-25, R.V.)

A sober reading of this record reveals what a tremendous sensation this preaching and healing work of Jesus must have created, and over what a wide area. Literally nothing like this had ever been heard of before, either in living memory or in the traditions of the past. The amount of excited speculation which must have taken place almost defies the imagination. The intention of these miracles of Jesus was well expressed some time later by that blind man, who, finding that the Jewish leaders would not accept Jesus' authority as at least "a prophet", exclaimed: "If this man were not from God, he could do nothing" (John 9:33, R.V.). The great signs Jesus performed were all intended to provide solid evidence that "this man must be from God". The next conclusion to be drawn was this: "If he has any message for us from God, we had better attend to it."

Now it is important to appreciate that the healings of Jesus, however startling, were never separated from his teaching. In Matthew's record the order is significantly "teaching . . . preaching the gospel of the kingdom, and healing . . .", suggesting

22

that the main purpose of his mission was the teaching and the preaching. The healings were a sign meant to reinforce the message.

The way the 5th chapter of Matthew opens is striking indeed: "And seeing the multitudes, Jesus went up into a mountain". How remarkable! What a wonderful opportunity to preach to multitudes! And Jesus deliberately leaves them and goes off up a mountain! The result was that "his disciples came unto him", probably not just the twelve, but all who wanted to learn. The work of the miraculous Spirit was to draw attention to the authority of the person of Jesus; but the true spiritual work of God in Jesus was in the gospel he preached, in words which, he said, "are not mine, but the words of him that sent me".

## The Spirit of Christ

There is another important conclusion concerning the experience of Jesus himself. The teaching and preaching he constantly undertook were not dependent on his miraculous powers. In other words his understanding of Divine truth was not miraculously created in his mind. The true source of his understanding becomes clear on occasions when he has to uphold the truth in the face of adversaries. At his temptation, three times he rebuts the subtle invitations to indulge his own desires or satisfy his own ambition, by declaring categorically, "It is written . . ." (Matthew 4:1-11). He condemns the Sadducees for their disbelief in the resurrection, saying, "Ye do err, not knowing the Scriptures, nor the power of God" (Mathew 22:29). His basic attitude is one of reverent acceptance of the Law, the Psalms and the Prophets.

It is not difficult to perceive how his understanding of the Word of God must have grown from his earliest years. As soon as he was old enough, Mary must have told him the secret of his birth. As a boy brought up in a devout Israelite atmosphere, his education in reading would be from the beginning in the holy Scriptures. Being "of quick understanding in the fear of the Lord" (Isaiah 11:3), how he must eagerly have searched those writings for the prophecies concerning himself! It is not really surprising therefore that at the age of twelve he should be found in the temple, astonishing the learned men there with his understanding, and saying to Mary and Joseph, "Didn't you know I would be in my

Father's house?'' The process of understanding would grow during the years he passed in Nazareth until he was ready, at the age of thirty, to undertake his mission. Then he would echo the words of the psalmist, as quoted by the apostle in Hebrews:

*"Sacrifice and offering thou wouldest not, but a body hast thou prepared me ... Then said I, Lo, I come (in the volume of the book it is written of me) to do thy will, O God."*

(Hebrews 10:5-6)

So what was written ''in the volume of the book'' influenced the mind of Jesus, who grew in understanding, wisdom and commitment.

It is important for us to appreciate that the decision of Jesus to do the will of God was his *own voluntary choice*. He was not forced into it by the fact that God was his Father, nor by any consciousness of a previous existence in heaven, nor indeed by the miraculous powers he possessed (an encouragement indeed, but so easy to exploit for his own advantage). The reason he was approved of God was that he ''loved righteousness, and hated iniquity; *therefore* God, even thy God, hath anointed thee ...'' (Hebrews 1:9). His knowledge of righteousness and iniquity came from the Word of God, which had so much power with him that he was able to say, in the crisis of his life, ''Not my will, but thine be done''.

Thus, in the person of Jesus, the two aspects of the work of the Spirit united: the miraculous, in the convincing signs he was able to give of his divine authority; and the ''spiritual'', in the development of his mind, or spirit, under the influence of the inspired Word of God. Moreover, this is the great significance of Jesus' example for us. What God desires of us is not a worship and obedience forced upon us, arising from fear of judgement, or a sense of bondage. God desires from us our own voluntary choice to serve Him according to the revelation of His Word, and not to serve ourselves. None can give Him greater pleasure than those who, influenced by the Spirit of His Word, deliberately choose to order their lives in His ways, instead of the ways of their own thoughts and desires.

## The disciples

After a time Jesus gave to his twelve disciples some of his own miraculous Spirit powers:

*"He called his twelve disciples together, and gave them power and authority over all devils, and to cure diseases. And he sent them to preach the kingdom of God and to heal the sick . . . And they departed, and went through the towns, preaching the gospel, and healing everywhere."* (Luke 9:1-2,6)

*"And they went out, and preached that men should repent . . . they cast out many devils, and anointed with oil many that were sick, and healed them."* (Mark 6:12-13)

A little later Jesus sent out seventy others in the same way:

*"After these things the Lord appointed other seventy also, and sent them two and two before his face into every city and place, whither he himself would come. Therefore said he unto them . . . Heal the sick . . . and say unto them, The kingdom of God is come nigh unto you . . . "* (Luke 10:1,9)

The pattern is the same as that followed by Jesus himself; the followers were to preach "repentance", the "gospel" and "the kingdom of God", and the authority of their word was supported by striking powers of healing. There are two comments of Jesus, however, upon the way these disciples reacted to the new powers given to them. When James and John observed the hostile attitude towards Jesus of the inhabitants of a Samaritan village, they wanted to use the powers they possessed in order to punish them:

*"When his disciples James and John saw this, they said, Lord, wilt thou that we command fire to come down from heaven, and consume them, even as Elias did?"*

But Jesus rebuked them, saying,

*"Ye know not what manner of spirit ye are of. For the Son of man is not come to destroy men's lives but to save them."* (Luke 9:52-56)*

---

*This saying is omitted in modern versions, with the acknowledgment that other ancient authorities contained it. It rings so true, however, that surely it must be authentic.

The disciples had not yet learned that there was more than one form of Spirit. They were eager to exercise their new powers, in defence of their Lord, but in the wrong way. They had been given the powers of healing, and they wanted to use them for judgement. They had not yet learned the importance of that other aspect of the Spirit, the spirit of their minds, which should have been desiring not to destroy but to save.

When the seventy came back, they

*". . . returned again with joy, saying, Lord, even the devils are subject unto us through thy name."*

Perhaps the rejoicing was rather more in the fact that *they* had powers to heal, than in the relief of suffering and the overcoming of evil. In his response Jesus foresaw the end of sin and evil: "I beheld Satan as lightning fall from heaven." He then adds this significant comment:

*"Notwithstanding in this rejoice not, that the spirits are subject unto you; but rather rejoice, because your names are written in heaven."*
(Luke 10:17-20)

Once more the miraculous powers of the Spirit are put in their true place; they were aids to the preaching, but did not ensure the salvation of those who possessed them.

From the Gospel records it would seem that these powers granted to Jesus' followers lasted for only a short time, like those of the seventy in the wilderness. Certainly little more is heard of them. It is indeed recorded that the disciples failed to heal an epileptic boy. When Jesus had healed him, the disciples asked him privately, "Why could not we cast it out?" Jesus replied, "Because of your little faith" (Matthew 17:14-20, R.V.). Was this why they asked him later, "Lord, increase our faith"? Did they want an increase in faith so that they could do more miracles? If so, this is why Jesus did not seem at first to answer their request, but finally said, "When ye shall have done all those things that are commanded you, say, We are unprofitable servants: we have done that which was our duty to do" (Luke 17:5,10). The lesson was clear, and still is: real faith comes from humility before God. This is the true manifestation of the Spirit.

26

## The Gift to the Apostles

The *fourth* intervention of the Spirit of God was in the bodily resurrection of Christ from the dead and in his ascension to heaven.

The proof that their Lord had literally "risen from the dead" was made known to his disciples by his appearances in ways which left them utterly convinced. They were invited to inspect the holes in his hands and in his side. "Handle me and see", he said to them; and he ate in their presence. Afterwards, Luke tells us, "he shewed himself alive after his passion by many proofs, appearing unto them by the space of forty days, and speaking the things concerning the kingdom of God" (Acts 1:3, R.V.).

This most significant of all manifestations of the power of the Spirit of God transformed the disciples from disillusioned and frightened men into convinced preachers of the gospel, willing to risk persecution, imprisonment and even death for their faith in Christ. They became witnesses of this great act of the Spirit, and also of Jesus' subsequent ascension to heaven, there to become "both Lord and Christ". It became the basis of their appeal for faith in him. Some time later the apostle Paul listed in his First Letter to the Corinthians, the numerous occasions when Christ had appeared to those who knew him, and he makes his resurrection the basis for the confidence of the faithful servants of God that He would raise them to a new life at the appointed time (1 Corinthians 15:1-20). Thus the resurrection of Christ becomes for the believers in the gospel what the Exodus had been to the nation of Israel: the great proof that their God had acted on their behalf and would continue to do so in faithfulness to His covenants of promise.

In their preaching the apostles could appeal to yet one more source of evidence. They were able to draw attention to the former work of the Spirit of God in the prophecies contained in the Law, the Psalms and the Prophets as proof that this great work of God had been long foretold. We know how they used Psalm 16 ("thou wilt not leave my soul in hell, nor suffer thine holy one to see corruption"). This type of appeal must have been very impressive to those devout Jews who were well acquainted with their sacred Scriptures. Once more the power of God's Spirit provided the basis for men to believe in the word prophesied and the word spoken.

## The Gift to the Apostles

The *fifth* intervention of the Spirit of God was in the granting to the apostles of special powers for their work of preaching, when Jesus had ascended to heaven.

He had promised this to them beforehand. The "Advocate" to come (a better rendering than "Comforter") was to "teach you all things and bring all things to your remembrance, whatsoever I have said unto you . . ."; it would "bear witness (R.V.) of me, and ye also shall bear witness"; it would "guide you into all truth . . . and will shew you things to come" (John 14:26; 15:26-27; 16:13). Luke records that as Jesus was about to leave them, he said:

*"Ye are witnesses of these things. And, behold, I send the promise of my Father upon you: but tarry ye in the city of Jerusalem, until ye be clothed* (R.V.) *with* **power from on high.***"*

(Luke 24:48-49)

*"John truly baptized with water; but ye shall be baptized with the Holy Spirit not many days hence . . . Ye shall receive power, after that the Holy Spirit is come upon you: and ye shall be witnesses unto me both in Jerusalem, and in all Judaea, and in Samaria, and unto the uttermost part of the earth."*          (Acts 1:5,8)

These promises received their initial fulfilment on the day of Pentecost. With the sound of a "rushing mighty wind" and the appearance of "cloven tongues like as of fire" upon each of the apostles,

*"they were all filled with the Holy Spirit and began to speak with other tongues, as the Spirit gave them utterance."*          (Acts 2:1-4)

This was their "baptism of the Holy Spirit". What a wonderful opportunity this was to proclaim Jesus of Nazareth as the Messiah, for "there were dwelling at Jerusalem Jews, devout men, out of every nation under heaven . . . and were confounded, because that every man heard them speak in his own language. And they were all amazed and marvelled . . ." (verses 5-7).

The range of the witness is shown by the national groups named: Parthians, Medes, Elamites, those inhabiting Mesopotamia,

Judaea, Cappadocia, Pontus, Asia, Phrygia, Pamphylia, Egypt, Libya and Rome, Cretans and Arabians. When they all returned home, they would carry with them the report of what they had seen and heard. So the gift of tongues at Pentecost in Jerusalem must have had repercussions throughout the Jewish communities of the Roman world. This initial witness by the power of the Holy Spirit prepared the way for the personal testimony of the apostles: first, Peter in Jerusalem, then Philip in Samaria, then Paul on his missionary journeys.

### The Spirit's Witness through the Apostles

The *sixth* divine intervention was in the witness to the gospel through the apostles, first beyond Jerusalem into Samaria, then to the Gentiles generally. The earliest record of this is the conclusion of the Gospel of Mark. After the ascension of Jesus, the apostles

> *"went forth, and preached everywhere, the Lord working with them, and* **confirming the word** *by the signs that followed."*
>
> (Mark 16:20, R.V.)

After the summary judgement upon Ananias and Sapphira, itself a confirmation that Peter was acting with the authority of God, we read that

> *"by the hands of the apostles were many signs and wonders wrought among the people (and ... believers were the more added to the Lord, multitudes both of men and women). Insomuch that they brought forth the sick into the streets ... There came also a multitude out of the cities round about unto Jerusalem, bringing sick folks, and them which were vexed with unclean spirits: and they were healed every one."*
>
> (Acts 5:12-16)

It is clear here that through the apostles was granted a demonstration of the power of the Spirit, such as had been witnessed two or three years earlier through Jesus, and with the same widespread effect. There must have been many there who remembered the healings of Jesus, and also some of his teaching. A similar manifestation occurred when, after the persecution of the believers in Jerusalem, the believers were "scattered abroad and went about preaching the word" (Acts 8:4). Philip was active in Samaria:

*"And the people with one accord gave heed unto those things which Philip spake ... **seeing the miracles which he did.** For unclean spirits ... came out of many ... and many taken with palsies, and that were lame, were healed. And there was great joy in that city."* (Acts 8:6-8)

The result was that "when they believed Philip, preaching the things concerning the kingdom of God, and the name of Jesus Christ, they were baptized, both men and women" (verse 12). Again, the signs were a witness to the authority of the word spoken. It was "the word" which was the means of salvation. One interesting feature is that Philip was not able to pass on his miraculous powers to others. It required the coming of the apostles, Peter and John, to achieve that (verses 14-18). This prompts the significant reflection that if those, like Philip, who had themselves received the gift of the Holy Spirit from the apostles, were unable to pass it on to others, then these special powers must have died out once the apostles were no longer there to transmit them.

## The Calling of Cornelius

From this case a number of valuable lessons can be learned. Cornelius was an officer in a cohort of Roman soldiers and was evidently a "God-fearer", that is a Gentile who frequented the synagogue services and acknowledged the God of Israel: "A devout man ... one that feared God ... gave much alms to the people, and prayed to God always" (Acts 10:1-2). What more could he possibly need? What follows is most instructive. This admirable man, whose prayers and alms were "come up for a memorial before God", still needed to hear through Peter "words whereby thou and all thy house shall be saved" (Acts 11:14). But Peter and his fellow Jews, believers in Christ though they were, yet needed convincing that it was right to welcome uncircumcised Gentiles into the faith. So God granted a special manifestation of the Spirit to achieve this.

The intervention was in four stages. First an angel appeared to Cornelius, telling him to send for Peter. It is worth noting that God did not supernaturally change the mind of Cornelius: He directed him to the source of instruction, to "the words" by which he was to be saved. Secondly, Peter received a vision which suggested that the distinction in the Law between "clean" and "unclean" was to be abolished: "What God has cleansed, that call not thou common" (10:9-16). This vision caused Peter great perplexity. Thirdly, "The Spirit said unto him, Behold, three men seek thee . . . Go with them, *nothing doubting* . . ." (verse 19). (The Spirit here is God acting through the power of His Spirit: more on this point later.) When Peter arrived at Cornelius' house, he showed he had learned the lesson: "God hath shewed me that I should not call any man common or unclean" (Acts 10:28). The fourth, and the most striking stage, occurred when "the Holy Spirit fell" on Cornelius and his listening household. To the astonishment of Peter and his Jewish companions, God had "poured out the gift of the Holy Spirit. For they heard them speak with tongues and magnify God" (verses 45-46). It was a miniature repetition of Pentecost. God had once again by His Holy Spirit provided a powerful witness, this time to Peter and his companions, that believing Gentiles were to be accepted into the body of Christ.

There are one or two interesting conclusions to be drawn from this divine intervention. It was not the miraculous gift which made Cornelius acceptable to God. It was his attitude of mind, ready to believe and to obey. Nor was it so much a witness to Cornelius and his household, though no doubt they were much encouraged. It was primarily a witness to Peter and his companions, to convince them that they were doing God's will in receiving these Gentiles. The prejudice had been great, and it needed a divine intervention to overcome it.

But the most interesting feature of all was Peter's reaction. After his initial astonishment Peter showed his understanding of essentials:

> *"Can any man forbid the water, that these should not be baptized . . .? And he* **commanded** *them to be baptized in the name of Jesus Christ."* (Acts 10:47-48, R.V.)

In other words, the miraculous gift of the Holy Spirit did not make Cornelius' baptism unnecessary, for it had no "moral" significance; that is, it did not reveal to him any truth which he had not already understood from the preaching of Peter. Of course it would be an encouragement to his faith, but no doubt, as in the case of the seventy in the wilderness, the effect was only temporary. Cornelius' salvation depended on his understanding of, and belief in the "words" spoken to him. This is an important conclusion, very relevant to some opinions held in our days.

## Peter and Paul

After Saul's conversion, there was relief from the persecution:

> *"Then had the churches rest throughout all Judaea and Galilee and Samaria, and were edified; and walking in the fear of the Lord, and in the comfort of the Holy Spirit, were multiplied. "* (Acts 9:31)

That is, having grown in understanding and living in reverence before God and His commandments, they were encouraged by the signs granted among them through the Holy Spirit. Two of these signs are immediately recorded: Peter healed Aeneas, the palsied man, at Lydda; and at Joppa he restored to life the lamented Dorcas, "a woman full of good works and almsdeeds which she did" (Acts 9:32-42). It is recorded of both places that "all that dwelt at Lydda ... turned to the Lord", and in Joppa "many believed in the Lord". So the believers would be encouraged in their life of faith. This was their "comfort of the Holy Spirit".

A similar power of witness was granted to the Apostle Paul. He remained some time with Barnabas at Iconium, "speaking boldly in the Lord, which *gave testimony* unto the word of his grace, and granted *signs and wonders* to be done by their hands" (Acts 14:3). Afterwards, when the vexed question of the admission of Gentiles to the body of believers without circumcision or keeping the Law, was debated in the council of Jerusalem, Barnabas and Paul declared "what miracles and wonders God had wrought among the Gentiles through them" (15:12). Apart from the isolated case of the twelve believers who had known only "the baptism of John" (the Baptist), and who received the gift of tongues when they were "baptized in the name of the Lord Jesus", the remainder of the Acts records no cases of miraculous powers. The emphasis is laid upon the preaching of the Word and the faith of the believers.

The whole subject is well summarised in the Epistle to the Hebrews:

*"How shall we escape, if we neglect so great salvation; which at the first began to be **spoken** by the Lord, and was confirmed unto us by them that heard him; God also **bearing them witness**, both with **signs and wonders** ... and **gifts of the Holy Spirit**, according to his own will?"* (Hebrews 2:3-4)

## The Gifts in the Ecclesias

This is the *seventh* occasion of divine intervention. In course of time, as the ecclesias increased in number and size through the preaching of the apostles and their fellow-workers, the situation arose in which some members had special Spirit gifts. The gifts could be rightly used or they could be abused. We are blessed to possess a section of the Apostle Paul's First Letter to the Corinthians (chapters 12-14), where he treats the subject in detail.

The Corinthians had evidently written to him about the matter, because of the disorder occurring in their ecclesias. He begins by asserting that although there are "diversities (varieties, R.S.V.) of gifts", there is only one Spirit and then clearly states what is to be his ruling principle in judging this matter:

*"But the manifestation of the Spirit is given to **each one** (R.V., that is, each one that has it) **to profit** withal (R.S.V., N.I.V., and other modern versions: for the common good)."*

(1 Corinthians 12:7)

Here is the vital point: Does the gift, or the use of it, promote the faith and understanding of the members? Repeatedly we shall find him returning to this point in this section of his Epistle. Paul then gives us a list of the gifts:

*"For to one is given through the Spirit the word of wisdom; and to another the word of knowledge, according to the same Spirit: to another faith, in the same Spirit; and to another gifts of healings, in the one Spirit; and to another workings of miracles; and to another prophecy; and to another discernings of spirits: to another divers kinds of tongues; and to another the interpretation of tongues: but all these worketh the one and the same Spirit, dividing to each one severally even as he (God, see verse 18) will."* (verses 8-11, R.V.)

Some of the gifts mentioned here we recognise at once. The gifts of healings, of working of miracles, of tongues and of the interpretation of tongues are similar to the signs already recounted in Acts. But what are we to make of Spirit gifts of wisdom, knowledge, faith and prophecy? These are qualities of the mind and the understanding. How precisely the gifts operated for those possessing them we do not know. One thing is clear, however: throughout Scripture God's servants are not represented as becoming wise or understanding or faithful because He has supernaturally injected these qualities into their minds, but because they have "set their minds on" (Romans 8) the words of His inspired servants. We may feel confident that those manifesting these particular gifts were men of spiritual understanding and faith, able under the blessing of God to edify the ecclesia. Perhaps the Spirit gift enhanced these qualities in suitable cases. The example of those who did construction work on the Tabernacle may afford a parallel (Exodus 31:3; 35:31).

Later in the same chapter Paul again describes the various gifts:

> *"God hath set some in the church, first apostles, secondly prophets, thirdly teachers, then miracles, then gifts of healings, helps, governments (administrators, R.S.V.), divers kinds of tongues."*
>
> (1 Corinthians 12:28, R.V.)

He seems here to be establishing an order of importance, in which "the ministry of the word" holds the foremost place, and miraculous powers are regarded as less important. This is consistent with his final exhortation: "Desire earnestly the greater gifts".

And yet, he says in chapter 13, there is something more important than any of these gifts, and that is love: that love which arises from the consciousness of one's own unworthiness, the great thanksgiving due to God for His abundant grace in the forgiveness of sins, and the recognition of the obligation to extend the same mercy to others. This is the basis of the mind of the Spirit. The various gifts will all "fail" and be "done away". But the need to understand the true nature of love, and to manifest it, will never pass away.

In chapter 14 the apostle deals with the practical problems created by the gift of tongues, and repeatedly makes clear what is his greatest concern. Here are a number of cases (from the R.V.):

Verse 1: *". . . desire spiritual gifts, but rather that ye may prophesy."*

Verse 3: *"He that prophesieth speaketh unto men to edification, and comfort, and consolation "* (note this definition of 'prophesying').

Verse 4: *"He that prophesieth edifieth the church."*

Verse 5: *". . . greater is he that prophesieth than he that speaketh with tongues, except he interpret, that the church may receive edifying."*

Verse 9: *". . . unless ye utter by the tongue speech easy to be understood . . ."*

Verse 12: *". . . since ye are zealous of spiritual gifts, seek that ye may abound unto the edifying of the church."*

Verse 18: *"I thank God, I speak with tongues more than you all: howbeit in the church I had rather speak five words with my understanding, that I might instruct others also, than ten thousand words in a tongue."*

Verse 22: *"Tongues are for a sign . . . to the unbelieving: but prophesying is for a sign, not to the unbelieving, but to them that believe."*

Verse 26: *". . . Let all things be done unto edifying."*

The main preoccupation of the apostle emerges clearly. The ecclesia is not an arena for the spectacular display of the gift of tongues, which so easily promote personal pride. That gift is but an aid to impress the unbelievers with the authority of the words spoken. Those who serve the ecclesia should have one aim: to edify the community, to build it up in understanding, to strengthen in faith and to console. The case of the gifts at Corinth illustrates once more that the powers granted were but signs to confirm the words of the preachers. For in the end it is not the ability to achieve the extraordinary which will save sinners from death, but "the words that are spirit and life" (John 6:63).

# 4

# THE SPIRIT AND THE WORD

SINCE the days of Jesus and the apostles the believers in God have received no direct communication from Him. For the last 1900 years there have been no open appearances of angels and no miraculous signs. No inspired prophets have arisen to give us a new revelation. Yet through these long centuries the faithful have not been abandoned, for the Word of God has been wonderfully preserved.

That deliberate counsel of God to commit to writing the revelation of His will for His people, first begun through Moses, then continued in the Law, the Psalms and the Prophets, was further continued in the apostolic age by the Gospels, the Acts, the Epistles and the Book of Revelation. So was formed the book of the Old and New Covenants, the Holy Scriptures. The great reverence among the Jews for the writings of the Old Testament, a reverence shared by Jesus and his apostles, was extended among the early ecclesias to the writings of the New.

Urquhart, in his *Inspiration and Accuracy of the Holy Scriptures* (pages 20-31), has a remarkable section in which he quotes extensively from Westcott's *Introduction to the Study of the Gospels*. The evidence is abundant that for the first three centuries the almost unanimous conviction was that "the Old and New Testaments were alike the Word of God". But it is significant that "this view has not grown. It is not a product of Christian evolution. It has been handed down right from apostolic times" (pages 20-31). The believers in the early ecclesias, says Urquhart, would never have been so emphatic about this, if the apostles themselves had not been equally emphatic. The writings which form our New Testament were added to the existing Law and Prophets, not because the leaders in those early days thought they should be preserved for their moral values, but *because they knew who had written them.*

So the faithful down the ages have not been left without help and guidance. They have had the written Word of God. Its power is firmly described by the Apostle Paul in his well-known saying to Timothy:

> *". . . the holy scriptures . . . are able to make thee wise unto salvation through faith which is in Christ Jesus. All scripture is given by inspiration of God (lit. is God-breathed) and is profitable for doctrine (teaching), for reproof, for correction, for instruction in righteousness: that the man of God may be complete, furnished completely unto every good work."* (2 Timothy 3:15-17, A.V. and R.V.)

What a tremendous declaration this is! If the writings we possess are "God-breathed", then His Spirit is in them. When that Spirit and its teachings are sincerely received, they have the power to create wisdom, to exert pressure to reprove and correct, and to make the believer "complete"! Here is the Spirit of God at work, not by miraculous means, but by the transforming power of the revelation—provided the mind of the reader is ready to accept it. How great should be *our* reverence for this God-breathed work, and how earnest our desire to understand it!

## True Knowledge of God

Sometimes the Bible is regarded as if it were just like the writings of men—only capable of giving information. "Bible knowledge" or "head knowledge", we are told, is not the same thing as "knowing God and his Son Jesus Christ". There is truth here, but the wrong conclusion is too often drawn. It is quite true, and it happens more frequently than we would like, that the doctrines (teachings) of the Bible can be understood and intellectually established, without the transforming effect they are designed to produce. But *where is the blame for that to be laid?* The Word of God is explicitly designed to enlighten, to create an understanding, to change the way of thinking; in brief, to "convert the soul". If this result is not achieved in individual cases, or indeed in communities, the fault is not in the Word which God has inspired, but in the men and women who fail to respond to it from their hearts. This is the crux of the matter. It has not been produced in such a form that it will automatically convert anyone who reads it. It is designed to elicit a willing and deliberate response. God wants men and women soberly and freely to choose Him to be their God, instead of choosing to live after their own desires. To this end He reveals His truth in all its facets, and appeals to the understanding, inviting all to share His thoughts, and His will, to perceive the difference between His Spirit and the spirit of the flesh.

The inevitable consequence of this approach is that all readers of the Word of God are invited to make a choice on the basis of understanding. So it has been all through the centuries of God's dealings with His people.

Moses to Israel:

*"See, I have set before thee this day life and good, and death and evil . . . therefore choose life . . . "* (Deuteronomy 30:15-19)

God to Israel:

*"Come, now, and let us reason together . . . If ye be willing and obedient, ye shall eat the good of the land: but if ye refuse and rebel, ye shall be devoured with the sword."* (Isaiah 1:18-20)

Jesus to all:

*"Whosoever heareth these sayings of mine, and doeth them"* shall endure, *"but everyone that heareth . . . and doeth them not"* shall perish. (Matthew 7:24-27)

(To hear, in Biblical language, implies to understand and to obey.) Hence the ceaseless exhortations in the apostolic writings to earnest obedience and faith, constantly implying a choice to be made.

One further matter: the Word of God does not cease to be so, or to lose its power to transform, just because men and women choose to reject it, or profess themselves "unable to accept it". The notion that "the Word of God is what it means to you", as some modern theologians hold, is quite inconsistent with the testimony of Scripture itself. The word of Ezekiel was God's Word for Israel,

*"whether they will hear or whether they will forbear"*
(Ezekiel 2:7; 3:11)

And so it has been for all generations since, including our own.

## The Word of Power

How could the Word of God be any other than "a word of power"? It has been created by the power of His Spirit upon chosen men. It is the full expression of His mind, His will, His Spirit, *Himself*, in contrast with the spirit and mind of human flesh. Every revelation of the spiritual mind of God is capable of exerting a profound effect upon the minds of men and women—upon one condition: that, like "the good seed" in the Parable of the Sower, they have "good and honest hearts". There is great instruction in this thought.

We have already noted the testimony of David (see page 17) in Psalm 19 to the power of the "law of the Lord" to "restore the soul", "make wise", "enlighten the eyes" and "warn", and in brief to "convert the soul." Let us notice particularly *where* this power is to be found: it is in "the testimony", "the precepts", "the commandment", "the judgements"—in other words in the separate, yet collective, commands and His comments upon them which God gave to His people. Now in David's day these "commands", summed up in "the commandment", were to be found in the written record, the Word of God itself: again, a powerful lesson for us.

Psalm 119 is another rich source of testimony to the power of the Word:

Verse 9:      A young man *"cleanses his way"* by *"taking heed . . . according to thy word . . ."*

Verse 11:     *"Thy word have I laid up in my heart, that I might not sin against thee."*

Verse 40:     *"Quicken me in thy righteousness* (that is, *thy salvation from sin*). *"*

Verse 50:     *"The word . . . is my comfort in mine affliction."*

Verse 92:     *"Unless thy law had been my delight, I should have perished in mine affliction."*

Verse 98:     *"Thou through thy commandments hast made me wiser than mine enemies . . . I have more understanding . . ."*

Verse 165:    Hence, *"great peace have they which love thy law, and nothing shall offend them (cause them to stumble)."*

39

The Psalmist prays that as a result of his "meditation" on the law, God will "quicken" him, "teach" him the statutes, make him to "understand", "strengthen" him, give him understanding, incline his heart unto the testimonies (verses 25-28, 33-36). He does not explain how God will do this, but the clear implication of the whole psalm is that such effects will arise from the psalmist's complete submission to the spirit of the Word of God. Such is the power of that Word to make the faithful servant "complete", as Paul says (2 Timothy 3:16). God will surely add whatever blessing He sees fit in His own way, but the faithful servant's attention is directed to the written word for his understanding and faith.

## The Word in the New Testament

The Apostle Paul's impressive testimony to the "God-breathed" Scriptures is reinforced in the New Testament by a large number of references to the various aspects of "the word". The following is a list, arranged under its various aspects. The reader is earnestly recommended to read each quotation very carefully indeed, trying to assess the importance of what is being asserted.

In a number of cases "the word" stands for "the gospel":

*"The* **word of the truth**, *the gospel of your salvation* ... *"*
(Ephesians 1:13)

*"The* **word of the truth** *of the gospel* ... " (Colossians 1:5)

*"The* **word of good tidings** *which was preached unto you."*
(1 Peter 1:25, R.V.)

*"(God)* ... *manifested* **his word in the message,** *wherewith I was intrusted."* (Titus 1:3, R.V.)

*"I (Jesus) pray* ... *for them also which shall believe on me* **through their** *(the apostles') word."* (John 17:20)

*"A workman that needeth not to be ashamed, handling aright the* **word of truth."** (2 Timothy 2:15, R.V.)

*"Remember them* ... *who have spoken unto you the* **word of God."** (Hebrews 13:7)

*"The* **word of the cross** *is* ... *the power of God."*
(1 Corinthians 1:18, R.V.; cf. Romans 1:16,
*"the* **gospel** *is the power of God unto salvation"*)

40

*"When any one heareth the **word of the kingdom**."*
(Matthew 13:18; cf. Luke 8:11,
*"the seed is **the word of God**"*)

The Word is in the teaching, which is to be understood and obeyed:

*"Ye became obedient from the heart to that **pattern of teaching** whereunto ye were delivered ..."*
(Romans 6:17, R.V. margin)

*"He that was sown upon the good ground, this is he that **heareth the word**, and **understandeth** it ..."*
(Matthew 13:23, R.V.)

*"Faith cometh by hearing, and hearing by **the word of God**."*
(Romans 10:17)

*"Wholesome words, even **the word of** our Lord Jesus Christ, and ... **the doctrine** which is according to godliness."*
(1 Timothy 6:3)

*"Holding to the **faithful word**, which is according to **the teaching** ..."*
(Titus 1:9)

*"I have given unto them **the words** which thou (God) gavest me (Jesus); and they have received them ..."*
(John 17:8)

*"Whoso **keepeth his** (Jesus') **word** ..."*
(1 John 2:5; cf. verse 3, *"we keep his commandments"*)

*"When ... persecution ariseth **because of the word** ..."*
(Matthew 13:21)

This Word of God is a word of power:

*"(God) begat us (R.V., brought us forth) **by the word of truth**."*
(James 1:18)

*"Receive with meekness **the implanted word** which is able to save your souls."*
(James 1:21, R.V.)

*"Having been begotten again, not of corruptible seed, but of incorruptible, **through the word of God**."*
(1 Peter 1:23, R.V.; cf. verse 25, *"**the word of good tidings** which was preached unto you"*)

*"Ye (disciples) are clean, **through the word** which I have spoken unto you."*
(John 15:3)

*"Sanctify them (disciples) through thy truth; **thy word is truth**."*
(John 17:17)

*"When ye received from us **the word of the message** ... ye accepted it ... as it is in truth, **the word of God**, which also **worketh** in you that believe."* (1 Thessalonians 2:13, R.V.)

*"The **word of God** is living, and active ..."*
(Hebrews 4:12, R.V.)

*"I commend you to God, and to **the word of his grace**, which is able to **build you up**, and to give you an inheritance among all them which are sanctified."* (Acts 20:32)

*"He that rejecteth me, and receiveth not my words, hath one that judgeth him: **the word that I have spoken**, the same shall **judge** him in the last day."* (John 12:48)

The Word of God or Christ is said to dwell or abide in the faithful:

*"Ye (Jews) have not his (God's) **word abiding in you** ..."*
(John 5:38)

*"If ye **abide in my word**, then are ye truly my disciples; and ye shall know the truth."* (John 8:31, R.V.)

*"**My** (Christ's) **word** hath not free **course** in you (Jews)."*
(John 8:37, R.V.)

*"If ye abide in me, and **my words abide in you** ..."*
(John 15:7)

*"Let the **word of Christ** dwell in you richly in all wisdom ..."*
(Colossians 3:16)

*"Young men ... ye are strong, and the **word of God abideth** in you."* (1 John 2:14)

The Word creates life and spirit:

*"He that heareth **my** (Jesus') **word**, and believeth on him that sent me, hath **everlasting life** ... (he) is passed from death unto life."*
(John 5:24)

*"It is the spirit that quickeneth; the flesh profiteth nothing: **the words** that I speak unto you, they are **spirit** and **they are life**."*
(John 6:63)

*"If a man **keep my word**, he shall never see death."*
(John 8:51, R.V.)

42

Certain conclusions arise from a careful reading of these quotations. God has sought to enlighten men not by some sudden revelation, some supernatural illumination, but by His truth which is expressed in His words, spoken and written down by inspired servants. His appeal is to the understanding, inviting the willing cooperation in obedient faith of those who will receive it. It is a dynamic word, for it can "work" in the believing, begetting a new outlook, creating faith, cleansing, building up, and sanctifying. It is the power of God unto salvation.

It is sometimes pointed out that the "word of God" in such passages refers not to the whole of the inspired Scriptures, but to God's saving truth. If the intention is to warn us against taking the inspired Bible as a "text book" and being satisfied with a knowledge of its facts, the point is valid.

But granted that "the word" often means the gospel, how are we in this distant age to discover what that truth is? There can be only one answer: since we have no inspired men to tell us, and no special revelation of our own, we must "search the scriptures" to find it. This our community has diligently tried to do for over 100 years. The message is described as the "good tidings concerning the kingdom of God and the name of Jesus Christ" (Acts 8:12, R.V., a description confirmed twice in the case of Paul's preaching at Rome, Acts 28:23,31). To enable us to understand the riches of this message, the whole of the inspired Scriptures, "God-breathed", have been provided for us. They are the collective record of the "wisdom that is from above".

## A Summary of the Gospel

It may help to try and summarise the main elements of these "good tidings". Throughout the ages God has been pursuing His purpose of taking out of the nations a people for His name. He revealed Himself first to Abraham and his seed with promise of everlasting blessing, and then amplified that revelation through the Law, the Prophets, His Son and the Apostles. Its unchanging truths are that God is holy and righteous, and that human flesh of itself produces only sin and death; but God in His desire to save, has manifested Himself in His Son in human flesh; that Son devoted himself to the will of the Father and conquered sin in himself, and so was able to make that sacrifice for sin which

43

provides the atonement; God, having demonstrated His righteousness in the essential sacrifice for sin, now in His mercy and grace forgives the sins of those who acknowledge these truths, obey His will and repent in faith of their ways. Granting them righteousness, He restores them to fellowship with Himself and promises them resurrection from the grave and immortality when His Kingdom is established at the second Coming of Christ.

Such eternal truths as these are meant to be understood and to be acted upon. Their aim is to effect a radical change in the minds of men and women. In those who accept them in humble sincerity they produce a new understanding, a wisdom that is "from above", and a deeper knowledge of God and of Christ which comes from sharing their thoughts and embracing their will. In other words this revelation produces in them "a new heart and a *new spirit*", called by God *"my spirit"* (Ezekiel 36:26,27—if of repentant Israel, how much more of the saints in Christ: Hebrews 10:14-17?).

Again it is a very enlightening exercise to read carefully through the New Testament descriptions of the understanding, the knowledge and the wisdom abundantly provided by God for His faithful:

The knowledge of the truth:

> *"If ye abide in my word* . . . *ye shall* **know the truth** . . . "
> (John 8:31,32, R.V.)

> *"The word of the truth of the gospel* . . . *ye heard* . . . *and* **knew the grace** *of God* . . . "
> (Colossians 1:5-6)

> *"God our Saviour* . . . *will have all men to be saved and to come unto the* **knowledge of the truth** . . . "
> (1 Timothy 2:3-4)

> *"Repentance unto the* **knowledge of the truth** . . . "
> (2 Timothy 2:25, R.V.)

> *"Ever learning and never able to come to the* **knowledge of the truth** . . . "
> (2 Timothy 3:7)

> *"Grace to you and peace be multiplied in the* **knowledge of God** *and of Jesus our Lord: seeing that his divine power hath granted unto us all things that pertain unto life and godliness, through the* **knowledge** *of him. "*
> (2 Peter 1:2, R.V.)

The renewing of your mind:

> *"Be not fashioned according to this world: but be ye **transformed by the renewing of your mind** ..."*
> (Romans 12:2, R.V.)

> *"Ye did not so **learn** Christ; if so be that ye **heard** him, and were **taught** in him, even as truth is in Jesus: that ye put away ... the old man ... corrupt after the lusts of deceit; and that ye be **renewed in the spirit of your mind**, and put on the **new man** ..."*
> (Ephesians 4:20-24, R.V.)

> *"Put on the new man, which is being **renewed unto knowledge** after the image of (God)."* (Colossians 3:10, R.V.)

> *"Have this **mind** in you, which was also in Christ Jesus: who ... humbled himself, becoming obedient ..."*
> (Philippians 2:1, R.V.)

> *"I delight in the law of God after **the inward man** ..."*
> (Romans 7:22)

> *"**With the mind** I myself serve the law of God"*
> (Romans 7:25)

> *"Our outward man is decaying, yet our **inward man** is renewed day by day"* (2 Corinthians 4:16)

> *"The hidden man of the heart, ... a meek and quiet **spirit** ..."*
> (1 Peter 3:4)

Your understanding being enlightened:

> *"The **light** of the gospel of the glory of Christ, who is the image of God ..."* (2 Corinthians 4:4, R.V.)

> *"The **light** of the **knowledge** of the glory of God in the face of Jesus ..."* (2 Corinthians 4:6)

> Paul prays that God *"may give unto you the **spirit of wisdom** and revelation in the **knowledge** of him: the eyes of your **understanding** being enlightened; that ye may **know** what is the hope of his calling ..."* (Ephesians 1:17-18)

> *"Till we all attain unto the unity of the faith, and of the **knowledge** of the Son of God, unto a full grown man ... the measure of the stature of the fulness of Christ ... no longer children ... but speaking truth in love, may grow up in all things into him ..."*
> (Ephesians 4:13-15, R.V.)

45

Paul prays *"that ye may be **filled** with the **knowledge** of (God's) will in all **spiritual wisdom** and **understanding** ... increasing in the **knowledge** of God ... "*

(Colossians 1:9-10, R.V.)

*"Their hearts may be comforted ... unto all riches of the full assurance of **understanding**, that they may **know** the mystery of God, even Christ, in whom are all the treasures of **wisdom** and **knowledge** hidden ... "* (Colossians 2:2-3, R.V.)

*"We know that the Son of God is come, and hath given us an **understanding**, that we may **know** him that is true, and we are in him that is true, even in his Son Jesus Christ. This is the true God, and **eternal life**."* (1 John 5:20)

*"Hereby do we know that we **know** him, if we **keep his commandments** ... "* (1 John 2:3)

*"Ye **know** the Father ... **the word of God** abideth in you."* (1 John 2:13-14, R.V.)

*"This is life eternal that they might **know** thee, the only true God, and Jesus Christ."* (John 17:3)

The numerous references in the above quotations to "knowing" and "knowledge" make a comment here essential. The Greek terms used imply much more than "knowing the facts" or being acquainted with the teaching, for they convey that state of mind which should arise out of the knowledge of these things. They imply the result of a sincere effort to live in obedience to the will of God as revealed in His Word—Paul calls it "truthing it in love" in Ephesians 4:15 above—and also that appreciation of the spiritual quality of the Divine Mind ("the Word" made flesh in Christ) in contrast with "the mind of the flesh". There is a process of spiritual growth here, indicated clearly by Paul in expressions like "that ye may *grow up* in all things unto him" (Ephesians 4:15) and *"increasing* in the knowledge of God" (Colossians 1:10).

But it remains essentially true that the growth of all such "spiritual wisdom and understanding" depends upon the understanding of, and hearty belief in, the fundamental teachings of Scripture; and that for these we must go to the written Word of God, His message for us today. The knowledge, understanding, discernment and wisdom, described so eloquently in the fore-going quotations, express the spirit of the mind that has been *renewed*, not by some direct action of God upon the heart, but by the spiritual power of the Word of God itself to "convert the soul" (Psalm 19:7). How wonderful it is that this Word of God still exists for us in all its fulness, still as powerful as ever to "work in them that believe".

### The Two Wisdoms

It may come as a surprise to some to learn that there is another "spirit" besides the Spirit of God. Consider the following:

*"Now we have received, not the **spirit of the world**, but the spirit which is of God . . . "* (1 Corinthians 2:12)

*". . . the **spirit** that now works in the children of **disobedience** . . . "* (Ephesians 2:2)

*". . . the spirit of truth, and the **spirit of error**."* (1 John 4:6)

The spirit of the world is the thinking of the human mind, in its "disobedience" and "error". Paul calls it "the god of this world". It is the expression, as Jesus told the Jews, of the "evil things that come from within, out of the heart of man" (Mark 7:20-23). It is the stubborn enemy of God, for "it is not subject to the law of God, neither indeed can be" (Romans 8:6-7).

The contrast between the spirit of the flesh and the Spirit of God is strikingly described by James. There are, he says, two wisdoms. One does not come from above, for it is "earthly, sensual, devilish" and produces "bitter envying and strife in your heart", with "confusion and every evil work".

Then the great contrast:

*"But the wisdom that is from above is first pure, then peaceable, gentle, and easy to be intreated, full of mercy and good fruits . . . without hypocrisy."*

And its fruit is

*"righteousness . . . sown in peace of them that make peace."* (James 3:14-18)

Now wisdom results from an understanding of truth, but understanding can only come as a result of knowledge; and the essential knowledge of God comes not as a direct action of His Spirit upon the heart, but by hearing, understanding and accepting the word of life.

The parable of the Sower conceals a remarkable confirmation of this. Concentrate on one case only, that of the "good seed"; put the three Gospel records together, and this is what appears (in the R.V.):

Matthew 13:23— *"he that* **heareth** *the word, and* **understandeth** *it* . . . *"*

Mark 4:20— *"such as* **hear** *the word, and* **accept** *it* . . . *"*

Luke 8:15— *"in an honest and good heart, having* **heard** *the word,* **hold it fast** *and bring forth fruit* **with patience.** *"*

An instructive sequence appears here. All three records stress the need to "hear" the Word, that is to pay attention and *listen* to it. Next comes the need for *understanding* what is heard. Then the supremely important stage: the Word must be *accepted*—not just known in its factual details, but received as sovereign in the believer's mind. Only then will he have the *patience* (that is, the endurance) to *hold it fast*, and bring forth the right fruit. Hearing, understanding, accepting, holding fast: what a remarkable description of the way the Word of God works in "a good and honest heart". By this process the sincere and devoted believer learns to recognise and to reject "the wisdom from beneath", the mind natural to human flesh, and to absorb "the wisdom from above" and to partake of the mind, or Spirit, of God.

It is by His Word, first spoken and then written down, that God has ever sought to awaken in the minds of men a sense of their own unworthiness, and an appreciation of His holiness and grace. For this, a process of understanding and transformation is essential. But the instrument God has chosen to *foster* His Spirit in the believer is fully able to perform that task. The Word of God, says Hebrews, is "living and active, and sharper than any two-edged sword, and piercing even to the dividing asunder of soul and spirit . . . and quick to discern the thoughts and intents of the heart" (Hebrews 4:12, R.V.); that is, the Word of God has the power, when reverently considered, to reveal a man to himself, to expose his need of redemption. It is also the means by which God "begets" new spiritual children:

*"Of his own will begat he us* **with the word of truth** *... "*
(James 1:18)

*"... having been* **begotten again**, *not of corruptible seed* (that is, not of blood, or of the will of the flesh), *but of incorruptible* (that is, of God), *through* **the word of God** *... And this is the* **word of good tidings** *which was preached unto you."*
(1 Peter 1:22-25, R.V.; John 1:13)

The effect upon the whole-hearted believer of this spiritually powerful word of God is that a new understanding arises within him. He realises the essential difference between "the mind of the flesh" and "the mind of the spirit" (Romans 8:6) and is "renewed in the spirit of his mind" (Ephesians 4:23); he is "transformed by the renewing of his mind" (Romans 12:2). There is a new spiritual creation within him called "the new man" (in contrast to "the old man" which is corrupt after the lusts of deceit). This new man is "created after God (after the likeness of God, N.I.V.; to be like God, R.S.V.), in righteousness and holiness of truth".

Thus is accomplished the work of the Holy Spirit in the minds and hearts of believers; not by a miraculous or independently direct influence, but by the searching, cleansing and sanctifying power of His Word to beget sons and daughters in His own spiritual image with their willing co-operation. "Sanctify them", prayed Jesus for the disciples, "in the truth; thy word is truth" (John 17:17)

# 5

## "THE SPIRIT" IN THE ENGLISH TEXT

AS we read on in the New Testament, the miraculous activity of the Spirit recedes into the background, and the "spiritual understanding" needed by the saints becomes more and more prominent. This leaves us with a problem: How are we to understand the manifestation or activity of the Spirit in any given passage? The first and most important answer must be, By the context; but here the English reader encounters a perplexing difficulty, for sometimes he will find "the Spirit" and at others "the spirit". Consider for example the following:

Romans 8:2—*"the law of the Spirit of life"* (in the original 1611 edition it was spirit, later altered to Spirit).

Romans 8:4—*"... who walk ... after the Spirit"* (in 1611, spirit; so R.V. today).

Romans 8:5—*"they that are after the Spirit (do mind) the things of the Spirit"* (A.V. 1611, spirit; later altered to Spirit).

Romans 8:6—*"the minding of the Spirit"* (A.V. margin).

Romans 8:9—*"Ye are ... in the Spirit ... "* (A.V. 1611, the spirit).

The later changes in the Authorised Version are all from spirit to Spirit. The Revised Standard Version and the New International Version use Spirit throughout. This is characteristic of modern versions.

In vain the ordinary reader will be assured by investigators that there is no difference between "Spirit" and "spirit". He cannot help feeling that a difference was intended; and so indeed it was, for the translators of the Scriptures were usually trinitarians and found subtle support for their doctrine in this device. Has the

50

distinction between Spirit and spirit any justification in the Greek manuscripts of the New Testament? <u>None at all, for there no distinction is made between words beginning with capital letters and others; the word is invariably *pneuma*.</u> There is an important conclusion from this: when in our English versions we find sometimes "Spirit" and at others "spirit", it is because the translators are *acting as interpreters* and are giving their own sense to the expressions.

## "The Holy Spirit" and "Holy Spirit"

There is, however, another feature of the Greek texts which does not seem to have received the attention it must surely deserve, and which can be of considerable help to us in understanding particular passages. It is distinctly surprising to discover that in a large number of cases the word "the" is not found: the text says not "the Holy Spirit" but "Holy Spirit"; not "the Spirit" but "Spirit" or "spirit". The theological grammarians will tell us that this is of little importance, since the article is often omitted, "especially after prepositions". But their grammatical rule may well be intended to serve their doctrinal purpose and should not be accepted without question. Especially is this so in the light of two reflections: Would the Spirit of God have been so indifferent to sense as to cause the inspired authors to write "*the* Spirit" or just "Spirit" indiscriminately? And still more must some explanation be sought when an examination of passages seems to reveal an underlying principle.

Let us try to illustrate: whenever the reference is to the direct will or activity of God or of Christ, it is always "*the* Holy Spirit" or "*the* Spirit":

> *"It was revealed unto (Simeon) by **the** Holy Spirit, that he should not see death, before he had seen the Lord's Christ."*
>
> (Luke 2:26)

The revelation was the direct act of God:

> *"**The** Holy Spirit by the mouth of David spake . . ."*
>
> (Acts 1:16)

> *"**The** Holy Spirit said, Separate me Barnabas and Saul."*
>
> (Acts 13:2)

51

> *"They were forbidden of the Holy Spirit to speak the word in Asia."*
> (Acts 16:6)

Cases such as these are usually quite clear.

In the case of the miraculous signs, if the emphasis is upon their *divine origin*, the article is used:

> *"Ye shall receive power, after that the Holy Spirit is come upon you."*
> (Acts 1:8)

> *"While Peter yet spake ... the Holy Spirit fell on (Cornelius and household) ... (Peter and companions) were astonished ... because that on the Gentiles also was poured out the gift of the Holy Spirit. For they heard them speak with tongues, and magnify God."*
> (Acts 10:44-46)

Peter had to be convinced that the phenomenon he was witnessing was the direct act of God upon Cornelius and his household.

But when the emphasis is rather upon the visible or audible manifestation, the article is frequently omitted:

> Paul to disciples of John Baptist: *"Did ye receive Holy Spirit when ye believed?"* They reply: *"Nay, we did not so much as hear whether Holy Spirit was given."* (Acts 19:2, R.V.)

Paul is enquiring whether they had received among themselves the practical evidence of the gift of the Holy Spirit. They reply: We did not know that had happened yet. After their baptism into Christ and the laying on of Paul's hands, *"the* Holy Spirit came on them" (the source of the power) "and they spake with tongues" (the phenomenon); they had received "Holy Spirit" (as verse 2).

Surprisingly perhaps in the case of Mary:

> *"The angel ... said unto her, Holy Spirit shall come upon thee, and power of Most High shall overshadow thee ... "* (no articles).
> (Luke 1:35)

The emphasis is upon the *effect* of this Spirit and power upon Mary.

> Pentecost: *"(the disciples) were all filled with Holy Spirit ... as the Spirit gave them utterance."* (Acts 2:4)

Here are both aspects in the same verse: the Holy Spirit of God was the source of the gift: Holy Spirit (no article) describes the effect.

The above observations do appear to provide some basis for understanding the presence or the absence of the article "the" before Holy Spirit and Spirit.*

---

*Some readers may feel concerned that they cannot tell from our English translations when "the" appears before "Holy Spirit" or "spirit" and when it does not. The fact has to be faced that in this matter the English does not help us. The student needs a Greek-English Interlinear New Testament (see Christadelphian Office lists). There the literal English translation underneath each line of the Greek text will read like this: "the Holy Spirit" or "(the) Holy Spirit", etc. Those who do not feel able to adopt this method will find in the Appendix a list of significant passages where the definite article "the" is omitted in the original Greek.

# 6

## "THE MIND OF THE SPIRIT"

THE examples quoted above are all cases where the Holy Spirit was manifested in power through effects which could be observed. Those who received it performed signs, spoke in tongues, or uttered the inspired word of God. But these powers are no longer evident amongst us. The *spiritual* quality of the mind of God and of Christ, and so of "the Spirit", is however as great a priority for the modern believers as it was for those in Israel and of apostolic times. This sense of "Spirit" appears in a number of New Testament passages, which are of the greatest importance for our understanding.

We begin with the passage in Romans 8 which is the key to them all. In the following extract it is essential to know what the apostle actually wrote, as distinct from the way his words are usually translated. The presence or absence of the definite article (the) will help our understanding:

*"The law of the Spirit of life in Christ Jesus has made me free from the law of sin and death."*                    (verse 2)

The "law of sin and death" is not so much a reference to the judgement pronounced in Eden, as a comment upon the fate of those who follow their own natural desires. They remain under the power of sin, and they perish for ever. But there is another influence which can operate in the minds of the believers. It is called "the Spirit"—note that its counterpart is "sin"—and it produces life. This is the contrast Paul will now expound. God has condemned sin where it is manifested—in flesh of sin—so that

*". . . the righteousness of the law might be fulfilled in us, who walk* (that is, *live*) *not after flesh (kata sarka) but after spirit (kata pneuma).*                    (verse 4)

Notice that the articles are omitted before "flesh" and "spirit". These are two spheres of influence to which men and women belong. The next verse shows where to look for the difference between them:

> *"For they that are after flesh (kata sarka) do mind the things of the flesh; but they that are after Spirit (kata pneuma) the things of the spirit."*　(verse 5)

"To mind" is of frequent occurrence in the New Testament. It is clearly expressed in Colossians 3:2—*"Set your mind* on things that are above, not on the things that are upon the earth" (R.V.; A.V. margin). To do that is to be "after Spirit". Note that the onus is on the believer. He must not expect God to change his mind for him. God has provided the revelation and the faithful must give their minds to it. The theme is continued and expounded in the verses which follow:

> *"They that are in flesh (en sarki) cannot please God. But ye are not in flesh (en sarki) but in spirit (en pneumati) . . . "*
> (Romans 8:8,9)

This is a valuable saying, for it shows clearly the meaning of "in flesh". Of course all believers have natures of flesh and blood, and so in that sense they all live "in the flesh". But clearly Paul is referring to their *minds*. They are not "in flesh", but "in spirit", if they have "set their minds" on the things of the Spirit. This is a great help to understanding what follows:

> *". . . if so be that Spirit of God (pneuma Theou) dwell in you. Now if any man have not Spirit of Christ (pneuma Christou), he is none of his."*　(verse 9)

> *"And if Christ be in you . . . the Spirit is life . . . "* (verse 10)

Very remarkable here is the fact that the article is twice omitted. Spirit-of-God is God-spirit.* This is evidently the same as Spirit-of-Christ or Christ-spirit; and this in turn is the same as "Christ in you". The spiritual quality of the mind of God and of Christ must be reflected in the faithful. Here is no externally injected Spirit, but the response of the believers to the revelation of the

---

*"The absence of the article suggests *quality*, and its presence definition" —A. Lukyn Williams, *Galatians* (Cambridge Greek Text for Schools, 1910), in Appendix Note F, p.152

quality of the Spirit of God. So Christ dwells in them if his words abide in them, if they keep his commandments and abide in his love (John 15:7,10). In this way Christ is formed in them; and the life of Jesus is manifested in their mortal flesh (Galatians 4:19; 2 Corinthians 4:11). This is the Spirit of Christ which the faithful must manifest, if they are to be truly of his people.

> *"But if the Spirit of him that raised up Jesus from the dead dwell in you, he that raised up Christ from the dead shall also quicken your mortal bodies through* (R.V.) *his Spirit that dwelleth in you."*
>
> (Romans 8:11)

The A.V. rendering "by his Spirit that dwelleth in you" has created confusion here by seeming to assert that the power responsible for Christ's resurrection is the same as the Spirit that dwells in the believers. The R.V. has, however, significantly altered "by" to "*through* his Spirit". The R.V. footnote reads: "Many ancient authorities read *because* of . . ." This understanding makes consistent sense of the whole passage: because the faithful manifest the mind of Christ, God will raise them also from the dead. It is interesting to note that in Romans 1:4 Paul asserts that Jesus "was declared to be the Son of God in power (R.V. margin) . . . by the resurrection of the dead", but it was "*according to a* (not *the*) *Spirit of holiness*". In other words, the reason why God was able righteously to raise Jesus was because His Son had manifested "a spirit of holiness": he had chosen to live not according to his own will, but the will of the Father. He had manifested the mind of the Spirit. So God will raise the faithful, if they have "God-Spirit" in them.

> *". . . if ye live after flesh (kata sarka), ye shall die; but if ye through spirit (pneumati) do mortify the deeds of the body, ye shall live."*
>
> (verse 13)

Where the A.V. has "through the spirit", Paul has no article and no preposition, but just the one word *pneumati*, the dative case of *pneuma* implying the instrument: "by Spirit"; that is, by his spiritual understanding which enables the believer to recognise the works of the flesh and to seek to avoid them.

> *"For as many as are led by Spirit-of-God (pneuma Theou: God-spirit, as in verse 9), they are sons of God."*     (verse 14)

As the Israelites were "led" in the wilderness by the cloud and the fire, so the faithful are "led" by "the light of the knowledge of the glory of God in the face of Jesus Christ" (2 Corinthians 4:6; more on this passage later). Their understanding of the Spirit of God renews their minds and gives direction to their lives.

> *"For ye have not received a spirit of bondage again unto fear* (R.V.)*; but . . . a spirit of adoption, whereby we cry . . . Father."*
>
> (verse 15)

Once more Paul has omitted the articles: it is not a bondage-spirit, but an adoption-spirit. These are clearly allusions to the attitude of mind of the faithful.

> *"The Spirit himself* (R.V.) *beareth witness with our spirit, that we are children of God . . ."* (verse 16)

This is a verse much used by those of evangelical persuasion who believe in the "inner witness of the Holy Spirit". What seems clear is that here are two different "spirits". By "our spirit" the apostle must be referring to "the mind of the spirit" which the believers are to develop. What then is this "Spirit" which "bears witness"? As always, we must let the Scriptures enlighten us. Here are the passages in the New Testament about this subject:

> *"The Comforter . . . which I will send unto you from the Father . . . he shall* **bear witness** *of me."* (John 15:26)

> *"(The apostles) preached . . . the Lord working with them . . .* **confirming** *the word with* **signs** *following."* (Mark 16:20)

> *"The Lord . . .* **bare witness** *unto the word of his grace, granting* **signs** *and* **wonders."** (Acts 14:3, R.V.)

> *"God . . .* **bare them witness** (Cornelius etc.)*, giving them the Holy Spirit, even as he did unto us."* (Acts 15:8)

> *"Salvation . . . spoken by the Lord . . . confirmed . . . by them that heard him; God . . .* **bearing them witness,** *both with signs and wonders and with divers miracles, and gifts of Holy Spirit."*
>
> (Hebrews 2:3-4)

The consistent testimony of these passages is that the Holy Spirit "bare witness" to the preaching of the apostles in the visible manifestations of power which were granted. In his Letter to the Romans, Paul was writing at a time when the Holy Spirit was still a tangible witness in the ecclesias. All Scriptural parallels suggest that Romans 8:16 refers to the same kind of manifestation. That is why it is distinguished from "our spirit". Paul writes "the Spirit *himself*" (R.V.) because this is the action of God or of Christ through the Holy Spirit.

The gist of this important passage (Romans 8:1-16) is clear. The "Spirit of God" and the "Spirit of Christ" in the saints consists in that ready reception of the thoughts and will of God which brings about in them that new birth "of Spirit" ("born of water and of spirit", *ex hudatos kai pneumatos*, John 3:5) which produces the "new creature". The knowledge and understanding of God's thoughts and His will must be sought in His Word of Truth. By the spiritual power inherent in that Word "Christ is formed in us" (as Paul puts it in Galatians 4:19), and "the life of Jesus is manifested in our mortal flesh" (2 Corinthians 4:11).

The other key passage is in Galatians 5:

> *"Walk in Spirit (pneumati*: no article, no preposition) . . . *the flesh lusteth against the Spirit, and the Spirit against the flesh: and these are contrary the one to the other: so that ye cannot do the things that ye would"*   (verses 16-17)

Notice that the arena of conflict between flesh and spirit lies in the "desires", that is *"the mind"*.

> *"But if ye are led by Spirit" (pneumati*: no article, no preposition; the parallel to *"led by God-Spirit"*, Romans 8:14).   (verse 18)

> *"The fruit of the spirit is love, joy, peace, longsuffering . . . "* (all activities of *the mind*).   (verse 22)

> *"They that are of Christ Jesus have crucified the flesh."*   (verse 24)

Compare similar expressions in John's writings: the faithful are *not of* the world or *of* the devil, but *of* God, *of* the Spirit, *of* the truth. They share the mind of Christ. Hence:

> *"If we live by Spirit (pneumati*, as above), *by Spirit (pneumati) let us also walk."*   (verse 25, R.V.)

The general teaching of these passages of Scripture is clear and important. Taken with other expressions used by the apostle

Paul, they show that truly believing men and women are "renewed in the spirit of their minds", "transformed by the renewing of their minds", "renewed unto knowledge after the image" of God; they have "the mind of the Spirit" and share the "Spirit of God" and the "Spirit of Christ". What is involved in this process is not just a stimulation of emotions, but a radical change in our personality, our character, upon the basis of our free choice. This essential work can only come about by our voluntary submission to the wisdom of God abundantly expressed in His Word of truth. By that Word of spiritual power our heart is enlightened, our spiritual wisdom and understanding are increased, and we become sons and daughters of God indeed. Applying a little differently Paul's expression, we may well exclaim with him: "Thanks be to God for his unspeakable gift!"

# Part II

# 7

## VARIOUS PASSAGES CONSIDERED

### WISDOM AND POWER

IN the early chapters of his First Letter to the Corinthians, the Apostle Paul has a great deal to say about wisdom and spirit. He reminds them that he had not been sent to preach the gospel in human words and wisdom, for that would empty "the cross of Christ" of all significance. He goes on:

> *"For the **word of the cross** is to them that are perishing foolishness; but unto us which are being saved it is **the power of God**."*　　　　　　　　　　(1 Corinthians 1:18, R.V.)

Here "the word of the cross" must be taken in relation to the apostle's assertion in the previous verse that Christ had sent him to "preach the gospel". The "word of the cross" is therefore the full significance of all that is proclaimed about the cross. And it is dynamic: that is, it has the power (*dunamis*) to save. Compare his assertion in Romans 1:16 that "the gospel is the power (*dunamis*) of God to salvation". We note the underlying principle that a divine word or teaching concerning salvation is not just neutral, or a matter of information only. When wholly received, it has a power of its own. We shall find this stressed still more in Ephesians.

The idea of a crucified Messiah ("Christ crucified") is foolishness to both Jews and Greeks, but:

> *"unto the called themselves* (R.V.m) *(it is) Christ (the) power of God and (the) wisdom of God."*　　　　　　　(verses 23-24)

Again the definite article is missing in both cases: *dunamis Theou* ... *sophia Theou*. It is divine power and divine wisdom, and *not* *human*.

This contrast between human wisdom and divine power is maintained in chapter 2. Again definite articles are omitted, as shown below:

> *"My speech and my preaching were not in persuasive words of (man's) wisdom, but in demonstration of (the) Spirit and of power (pneumatos kai dunameōs): that your faith should not stand in (the) wisdom of men (en sophia anthropou) but in (the) power of God (en dunamei Theou)."*            (verse 4, R.V.)

In the context of his whole discussion, Paul here is clearly not thinking of the spirit and power in any miraculous sense. His subject is his "speech" and "preaching". He has already told us that the preaching of the cross has wisdom and power. Here he adds that it has "spirit". The divine quality arises because it reflects not the mind, or spirit, of man, but the mind, or Spirit, of God.

The contrast occurs again:

> *" ... we speak wisdom ... yet a wisdom not of this world, nor of the rulers of this world ... but we speak (God's) wisdom in a mystery ..."*            (verse 6, R.V.)

The "divine wisdom" was hidden from the rulers of this world, but has now been revealed (the mystery, or secret, has now been made plain):

> *"Unto us God revealed it* (R.V.m) *through the Spirit: for the Spirit searcheth all things, yea, the deep things of God ..."*
>            (verse 10, R.V.)

We have already noticed that whenever *"the* Spirit" is active, it is a reference to the direct initiative of God or of Christ (see pages 51-53). The apostle shows what he has in mind by a direct contrast with the case of man:

> *"For who among men knoweth the things of a man, save the spirit of the man, which is in him?"*            (verse 11, R.V.)

Here "the spirit of the man" is his mind, by which he is conscious of himself, of his experience, his desires and his purposes. In the same way,

> *" ... the things of God none knoweth, save the Spirit of God."*

Here the Spirit of God is His mind, the expression of His spiritual nature, in His will and purpose. No man could know about this of his own ability. But God has revealed it: it is the divine wisdom. So,

> *"We have received, not the spirit of the world, but the spirit which is of God; that we might know the things that are freely given to us of God."* (verse 12)

Here again we have the same contrast between worldly wisdom and the divine wisdom. It is interesting to note that the translators of the A.V. and the R.V. print "spirit" in both cases, showing that they understood "the spirit of God" to mean the divine mind in its wisdom. Significantly all modern versions print "the Spirit of God", no doubt wishing to support their doctrine of "the Holy Spirit".

> *"Which things also we speak, not in words which man's wisdom teacheth, but which (the) Spirit teacheth"* (A.V. has *Holy Spirit*).
> (verse 13, R.V.)

## Natural and Spiritual

So this divine wisdom or spirit is expressed in the words spoken (and of course written) by the apostles.

The conclusion of the verse, "comparing spiritual things with spiritual", has received differing translations. The R.V. margin has: "interpreting spiritual things to spiritual men", which at least has the considerable merit of agreeing precisely with what Paul now proceeds to say:

> *"The natural man receiveth not the things of the Spirit of God: for they are foolishness unto him: neither can he know them, because they are spiritually discerned."* (verse 14)

"The things of the Spirit of God" are the truths of the gospel which God has revealed by His Spirit through His "apostles and prophets". The "natural man" cannot estimate them at their true value, for his is "the mind of the flesh". But, says Paul,

> *"He that is spiritual judgeth* (margin, *discerneth*) *all things . . . "*
> (verse 15)

"All things"—that is, all the truths relevant to his salvation which God has revealed. But this "judging" is performed by the *mind.* The "spiritual man" is not then one who has received

62

some special direct gift from the Holy Spirit; he is one who, having "set his mind" (Romans 8:5) to understand and absorb the divine wisdom through the truths God has revealed, is in process of developing the "mind of the spirit". In fact, concludes the apostle, "we have the mind of Christ".

Paul's theme in the second chapter of the First Letter to the Corinthians is the sheer contrast between two wisdoms: one human and the other divine. The divine wisdom has become available to mankind because God has revealed it by His Spirit, "in words which the Holy Spirit teacheth". The truths of God's revelation are therefore Spirit, and they are powerful in those who sincerely receive them. In the "good and honest heart" they are the means whereby the believing disciple is able to assimilate the mind of Christ.

## "SEALED WITH THE HOLY SPIRIT OF PROMISE"

THE chapter from Corinthians we have just considered forms an excellent basis for understanding the allusions Paul makes to the work of the Spirit in his Letter to the Ephesians. In fact it is an essential basis, for in Ephesians Paul assumes the foundation truths about human and divine wisdom, the spirit of man and the spirit of God, without re-stating them. The reader of Ephesians needs to keep them in mind. The failure to do this has produced erroneous interpretations of Paul's sayings about the Spirit.

> *"(Ye Ephesians) having heard the word of the truth, the gospel of your salvation, —in (Christ), having also believed, ye were sealed with the Holy Spirit of promise, which is an earnest of our inheritance, unto the redemption of God's own possession, unto the praise of his glory".*
> (Ephesians 1:13-14, R.V.)

What was this "sealing with the Holy Spirit"? There are two important clues: it was "the Holy Spirit *of promise*", and it was "an earnest" of a fuller inheritance to come.

"The promise" is reported in two important passages from Luke. The concluding verses of his Gospel and the first verses of Acts record how Jesus appeared to his disciples after his resurrection and told them that they were to act as witnesses to his preaching, his death and resurrection. Then he promised them a help in their task:

63

*"Behold, I send* **the promise of my Father** *upon you: but tarry ye in the city of Jerusalem, until ye be clothed* (R.V.) **with power** *from on high. "* (Luke 24:49)

*"Being assembled together* . . . *he charged them not to depart from Jerusalem, but to wait for* **the promise of the Father**, *which, said he, ye heard from me* . . . *ye shall be baptized with the Holy Spirit not many days hence* . . . *Ye shall receive* **power**, *when the Holy Spirit is come upon you: and ye shall be my witnesses* . . . "
(Acts 1:4,5,8, R.V.)

The promise was clearly fulfilled on the day of Pentecost, both in the message of salvation in Christ, here proclaimed for the first time, and in the manner of it: the gift of tongues, when *"the* Holy Spirit" came upon them. (The use of the article shows that the initiative was from God Himself while the effect upon them, the gift itself, is described as "Holy Spirit".) This gift of the Holy Spirit was a guarantee ("earnest") in apostolic days of the still greater manifestation of Spirit nature and power ("the powers of the age to come", Hebrews 6:5) to be granted to the saints when they receive the fulness of their inheritance in the Kingdom of God: "The guarantee of our inheritance until we obtain possession of it" (R.S.V.). A seal conveys the authority of its owner. So the apostles were "sealed" by this Spirit gift: God authorised their witness as coming with His own approval and power. He "confirmed their word" by the signs which accompanied their preaching (see comments on Romans 8:16, page 57).

One important principle arises from the order of events. The Ephesians first "heard the word of the truth, the gospel" of their salvation; then they believed it. Only after that did they receive "the Holy Spirit of promise". The Scriptural order is always so. Clearly the Ephesians did not need the Holy Spirit to enable them to believe, as so many modern theologians would contend. Their salvation depended not upon some miraculous gift, but on their careful attention to, and belief in, "the word of the truth".

### "The earnest of the spirit"
It seems evident, however, that the ideas of "sealing" and "the earnest (guarantee) of the spirit" can have a further application. Paul wrote to the Corinthians:

*"Now he that stablisheth us with you in Christ, and anointed us, is God; who also sealed us, and gave us the earnest of the Spirit in our hearts."* (2 Corinthians 1:21-22, R.V.)

What seems to distinguish this paragraph from the similar one in Ephesians is that this "earnest of the spirit" is "in our hearts", which does not sound like an allusion to the miraculous gifts. Further, "hearts" in both Old and New Testament, conveys more than the feelings, for it involves the understanding. "In our hearts" is therefore equivalent to "in our *minds*".

The believers' understanding and manifestation of the Spirit of God, even in the days of their flesh, is a guarantee of that greater understanding and communion with the Father which will be their inheritance in the Kingdom. In this sense they are "sealed" spiritually with the quality of God's own Spirit, since they manifest His will and His ways. Like the redeemed in the Revelation, they are "sealed in their foreheads", marked out as God's people by their faithful and spiritual service (7:3). It is in this way that God has "anointed" them. Anointing in Bible times was the sign of appointment to the special service of king or of prophet. The saints have been chosen by God to be heirs of His Kingdom, and their reflection of His Spirit in understanding and wisdom is both a sign of His choice and a guarantee of the spiritual fulness to come.

## "IN ONE SPIRIT"

NOW we shall continue in Ephesians:

Paul prayed *"that the God of our Lord Jesus Christ, the Father of glory, may give unto you a spirit of wisdom and revelation in (the) knowledge of him; having the eyes of your heart enlightened, that ye may know what is the hope of his calling, what the riches of the glory of his inheritance in the saints, and what the exceeding greatness of his power to usward who believe, according to that working of the strength of his might which he wrought in Christ, when he raised him from the dead, and made him to sit at his right hand ... far above all rule ... and he put all things in subjection under his feet ... "* (Ephesians 1:17-19, R.V.)

The apostle's prayer is that God will grant the Ephesians "a spirit of wisdom" in their knowledge of God: that is, having understood through His revelation the truths of the gospel, they will cultivate the divine wisdom and reject the wisdom of the world. This will come about by "the eyes of their heart being enlightened" (the A.V. "understanding" is based on a reading now generally rejected). In Scripture the heart represents the mind as well. The "seeing" is by *spiritual* discernment (see 1 Corinthians 2:14, page 62), and enlightenment must be of the understanding. These are functions of the mind. As a result of this understanding the believers will be convinced of the hope of life which is theirs by their belief of the gospel; they will appreciate their glorious inheritance in the Kingdom to come (to say nothing of their present inheritance of glory—see comment on Ephesians 3:20 ff.); and they will realise that the God of almighty power who raised Jesus from the dead and exalted him to His own right hand with authority over all things in heaven and in earth, is indeed *their* God and Father, who will do for them all that He sees is needed. This is a variation of Paul's theme at the conclusion of Romans 8: "Nothing can separate us from the love of God."

In this passage Paul is concerned with the spirit of the mind, in knowledge, enlightenment and wisdom. He wishes to reassure the faithful that God will use His great power on their behalf to ensure their inheritance of the Kingdom. Paul does not specify how God will do this. He is urging the Ephesians to trust in the fact, and to have confidence that He will eventually raise His saints from the dead if necessary, as He raised His Son.

In Ephesians 2 there are two references to "the Spirit". They are suitably introduced by verse 10:

*"We are (God's) workmanship, created in Christ Jesus (en Christō Jesou) for good works"*.

What the apostle means by "*in* Christ Jesus" will appear later. In chapter 4 he says, "The new man, which *after God* is created in righteousness and holiness of truth" (verse 24, R.V.), which the R.S.V. paraphrases as "after the likeness of God". It is of course a spiritual likeness, in which the thoughts and will of God are manifested in the minds of the saints. To be "in Christ" is therefore not limited to knowing and believing the gospel and being baptized, essential as these are. It involves reflecting "the mind of Christ" (1 Corinthians 2:16), the "Christ-spirit" (Romans 8:9), without which we do not really belong to him.

In verses 13-18 Paul stresses how, by his sacrifice, Christ had healed the breach between Jew and Gentile:

*"In Christ Jesus ye that once were far off (Gentiles) are made nigh by the blood of Christ ..."*

He has created *"in **himself** of (the) twain one new man, so making peace; and that he might reconcile both unto God **in one body** by the cross ..."*                              (verses 15,16)

The "one body" is evidently the united community of believers, whether Jews or Gentiles originally. This is clear from Paul's assertion that the Gentile believers are now "fellow citizens with the saints, and of the household of God ... " (verse 19), since they are built upon the same foundation teaching of the "apostles and prophets" and the same fundamental understanding of the salvation of God in Christ.

But what is it which could achieve this precious unity among people of such diverse origins? Will doctrinal agreement alone preserve it? That there *is* agreement about essential teaching in this new community is clearly shown by their being "built upon the foundation of the apostles and prophets", that is upon their teaching. But something more is needed, and Paul proceeds to tell us what it is:

*"... through (Christ) we both (Jews and Gentiles) have our access in **one** Spirit (en eni pneumati) unto the Father."*

(verse 18, R.V.)

The A.V. "*by* one Spirit" tends to mislead, suggesting that God accomplishes this independently by the power of His Spirit. But the preposition is *en*, and the sense is "*in*", meaning location or sphere of influence. The "one spirit" is the "mind of Christ", based on that humility and lowliness of mind which Paul recommends to the Philippians when he exhorts them to:

*"be of the same mind, having the same love, being of one accord, of one mind; doing nothing through faction or through vainglory, but in lowliness of mind ... Have this **mind in you**, which was also in Christ Jesus: who ... humbled himself ..."*

(Philippians 2:2-8, R.V.)

## "The mind of Christ"
How remarkable that "mind" occurs four times in this short

67

passage! Here is the "one spirit", the mind of Christ manifested in the faithful, which is the essential guarantee that men and women of diverse characteristics will be able to inherit harmoniously the same spiritual household.

In chapter 4 Paul writes again about it:

*"I ... beseech you to walk worthily of (your) calling ... with all lowliness and meekness, with longsuffering, forbearing one another in love; giving diligence to keep the* **unity of the Spirit** *in the bond of peace. There is one body, and* **one Spirit** *... "*

(Ephesians 4:1-4, R.V.)

This is not just a "unity of spirit" among the believers, because they are all of the same mind. It is a unity of *the* Spirit, because it issues from the mind of God Himself, being the moral expression of His Spirit, manifested in His people. Hence, says Paul, there is "one spirit", one spiritual quality, first in God, then in Christ, then in his followers.

In this connection the reference to "the bond of peace" is quite fundamental. This is no mere human "peaceableness", an innate "good nature" which is loth to quarrel with anyone. It arises in three stages from the clear teaching of Scripture.

First, as ignorant creatures of flesh, we are inevitably drawn to follow our own will, think our own thoughts and seek to satisfy our own desires: we are subject to the law of sin and death.

Second, we come to acknowledge the truth of the divine judgement upon ourselves; and, repenting of our ways, we seek the forgiveness of our sins.

Thirdly, God in the riches of His grace, forgives the sins of those who truly repent, and restores them to fellowship with Himself through the redemption achieved in His Son.

So we are "reconciled to God through the death of His Son" and have "peace with God" (Romans 5:10,1). We are no longer "alienated and enemies in our mind" (Colossians 1:21), but being convinced of God's gracious favour towards us, have a sense of peace with Him. The sense of "peace with God" is the "bond" which preserves the "unity of the spirit" among those who believe, for the truth of God has shown them that, eschewing all pride, they have no rights and no claims of themselves, but owe all to the mercy of God. Hence the "lowliness and meekness with longsuffering" which forms the basis of the apostle's exhortation to preserve "the unity of the spirit" among them. It is an essential condition for its preservation.

One further comment is needed:

*"There is one body, and one Spirit, even as ye are called in one hope of your calling; one Lord, one faith, one baptism, one God and Father of all, who is above all, and through all, and in you all. "*

(Ephesians 4:4-6)

It is clear that a considerable amount of doctrine, that is teaching, lies behind this passage. This is no mere emotional commitment to God. We have already treated the "one Spirit". Here we have in addition a calling, hope, faith, baptism, Jesus as the one Lord, and God as Father. All these terms have their meanings explained in various passages of Scripture. Here is a worship of the "one God and Father" based upon a knowledge and understanding of His revelation in His Word of truth.

We were led into chapter 4 of Ephesians by Paul's expressions "in one body . . . in one Spirit" of chapter 2. We must return there to notice the apostle's conclusion:

*"Being built upon the foundation of the apostles and prophets, Christ Jesus himself being the chief corner stone; in whom each several building, fitly framed together, groweth into a holy temple in the Lord; in whom ye also are builded together for a habitation of God in (the) Spirit (en pneumati). "* (Ephesians 2:20-22, R.V.)

The A.V. has "through the Spirit". The apostle wrote two words: "in Spirit". This passage is typical of a number where in the A.V. a result is said to be achieved "by" or "through" the Spirit. Such translations give the strong impression that "the Spirit" is the direct agent or instrument in the operation. This leads naturally to a belief in the independent action of the Spirit in the believer.

However, the Greek preposition used in these cases is mostly *en*. Vine, in his *Expository Dictionary of New Testament Words* (Part III, page 259) says it is the most common preposition of all, with "several meanings", but underlying them all is the sense of "location", of place and time. A reference to Young's *Concordance* reveals that *en* is used about 2,500 times in the New Testament.

In about 90% of cases it conveys the idea of location: "in", "at", or "among", and "at" of time. In only 10% of cases is it rendered "by", "with" or "through" in the Authorised Version. It is a striking fact, however, that in nearly every case involving "the Spirit" or "the Holy Spirit" the Revised Version has altered "by" or "with" to "in" or "through" the Spirit. In other words the instrumental sense has been deliberately weakened in order to convey rather a state or a condition. So, to look again at the quotation above: "for a habitation of God *in* the Spirit", says the R.V. (Ephesians 2:22). But Paul wrote *en pneumati* with no article: "in Spirit" or "in spirit"; that is to say, the way God dwells in us is by the presence of His Spirit in us, not by its direct action. If we share His thoughts and embrace His will, we share His Spirit, so He dwells in His saints "in Spirit". There is a similar expression in chapter 5:

> "... *be ye not foolish, but understand what the will of the Lord is.*
> *And be not drunken with wine (oinō, by wine), but be filled with the*
> *Spirit.*"                                    (Ephesians 5:17-20, R.V.)

—a passage often appealed to by those who favour spontaneous emotional reactions. But Paul wrote two words ony: be filled *en pneumati*, in Spirit; or as the R.V. margin actually says, "in spirit". Observe the contrast between *oinō* (the 'instrumental' case of the noun, "by wine", the means by which drunkenness is caused) and *en pneumati*, the state or condition of Spirit.

Paul goes on to show us what are the signs of the presence of this "spirit" in the saints: "*giving thanks* always for all things in the name of our Lord Jesus Christ ... *subjecting* yourselves one to another in the fear of Christ" (5:20-21, R.V.). In other words, thanksgiving and humility are two of the signs of the presence of the Spirit in us. They show that we have begun to understand the spiritual character of God and are trying, through the power and influence of His Word, to encourage its growth in themselves.

## "STRENGTHENED WITH POWER"

WE consider next the longest and most substantial of Paul's treatments of the Spirit in Ephesians:

> Paul prayed "*that (God) would grant you, according to the riches*
> *of his glory, that ye may be* **strengthened with power through**

*his Spirit in the inward man; that Christ may dwell in your hearts through faith; to the end that ye, being rooted and grounded in love, may be strong to apprehend with all the saints what is the breadth, and length, and height, and depth, and to know the love of Christ which passeth knowledge, that ye may be filled unto all the fulness of God. Now unto him that is able to do exceeding abundantly above all that we ask or think, according to the power that worketh in us, unto him be the glory . . . "* (Ephesians 3:16-21, R.V.)

This is a very important passage, raising some vital issues. How are the faithful "strengthened with power" through God's Spirit? What is this "power that worketh in us"? What is its source and how does it work? One principle is important: the significance of "power" and "Spirit", and of their "working" in the saints, must not be imported into this passage from elsewhere. It must be sought in the passage itself, in harmony with the rest of Scripture. We must examine with great care all that Paul says here.

First, why does he begin by saying that the work of God "through His Spirit" is "according to the riches of his glory"? What glory is this? Not the supreme power by which He accomplished the Exodus and the miraculous signs in the earth, but in the glory of His spiritual nature, His very character, which He Himself declared to Israel:

*"The Lord, a God full of compassion and gracious . . . plenteous in mercy and truth; keeping mercy for thousands, forgiving iniquity and transgression and sin: and that will by no means clear the guilty . . . "*
(Exodus 34:6-7, R.V.)

Here is the spiritual glory of God, His very being, a combination of truth, mercy and holiness.

"The Deity is wisdom as well as Power. Hence the Divine Nature is a moral nature, as well as substantial; so that His moral attributes are constituents of His glory, equally with those of His substance, in its essentiality and power."
(John Thomas, *Eureka*, Vol. I, Sect. II, p. 105, Orig. Ed.)

This is the moral and spiritual glory which God strove to reproduce in Israel, "the people for his possession", and which they rejected. So have all nations ever since, for "all have sinned and fall short of the glory of God" (Romans 3:23). This divine glory was, however, manifested at last in the person of His only begotten Son, for, says John, "the Word (that is the very mind of God) was made flesh, and tabernacled (R.V.margin) among us, (and we beheld his glory, glory as of the only begotten from the Father), full of grace and truth" (1:14). The bracket in the A.V. and R.V., and the altered order of the R.S.V., are meant to suggest that the glory of Christ was the fact of his being his Father's only begotten Son. Of course it was, but equally it arose from his being "full of grace and truth". Christ shared the spiritual glory of God in his words and his ways.

Paul has a helpful passage in 2 Corinthians. "The minds of the unbelieving", he says, have been blinded by "the god of this world". This is a valuable starting point for understanding what he says next. His subject is men's "minds", their thinking and understanding, perverted by "the wisdom of the world" (see 1 Corinthians 1 and 2). But the truly understanding mind has received "the light of the gospel of *the glory* of Christ". Notice that the glory of Christ is revealed through the light, or enlightenment, which the knowledge of the gospel brings. By this enlightenment the faithful perceive Christ as "the *image* of God", that is of course the spiritual reflection of God. For:

*"God . . . shined in our hearts, to give the light of **the knowledge** of the glory of God in the face of Jesus Christ."*

(2 Corinthians 4:6)

The "face" of Jesus is surely more than that part of him where the divine glory was reflected at the Transfiguration. It stands for his head, the place of understanding. He reflected God's spiritual character and we come to understand this by our knowledge of him. So, as the apostle was first concerned with minds which were blinded, he now deals with minds enlightened by their knowledge of the glory of God in Christ.

But, Paul goes on, "we have this treasure in earthen vessels". The treasure is the knowledge of the glory; the earthen vessels are the frailties of our minds. This teaches us that the *power* to enlighten, to transform, comes not from us, but from God. So the knowledge of the glory of God is powerful (as we shall see). It takes the form of "the life of Jesus" being "manifested in our mortal flesh". There is the glory of God in the saints. And it *works*: for, alluding to the sufferings of the preachers of the gospel,

Paul adds:

*"So then death worketh in us, but* **life** *in you."* (verse 12)

So "life" *works* in the believers. But the life is the manifestation of "the life of Jesus", the glory of God.

This then is why Paul commences his important passage in Ephesians 3 with the words "according to the riches of his glory". He is going to talk about the manifestation of the Spirit of God in the minds of the faithful. He goes on:

*"that ye may be strengthened with power through his Spirit in the inward man."* (verse 16, R.V.)

This is a valuable comment, for it tells us where the Spirit is: "in the inner man". The meaning of this is clearly expressed by Paul when he describes the conflict between his desire to do good and the weakness of his human nature:

*"I delight in the law of God after the* **inward man** *... But I see another law in my members, warring against the law of* **my mind** *... So then with* **the mind** *I myself serve the law of God ..."* (Romans 7:22-25)

## "That Christ may dwell in your hearts"

The manifestation of the Spirit of God is therefore in the mind of the believer. Being "born again", he is a "new creature", having been "renewed in the spirit of his mind" (Ephesians 4:23). The result is:

*"that* **Christ** *may dwell in your hearts through faith."* (Ephesians 3:17)

The "spirit in the inner man" is "Christ in their hearts". Remembering that in Scripture "the heart" always implies a large measure of the will and the understanding, we perceive the parallel. That Christ "dwells" or "abides" in us when his words abide in us, is a clear teaching in the writings of the Apostle John (John 15:7,10; 14:23). To the Galatians Paul expresses his anxiety over their lack of spiritual progress, "until Christ be formed in you"; and concerning himself, "Christ liveth in me ... the life I now live in the flesh I live in faith, the faith which is in the Son of God". He sums up by saying, "God sent forth the Spirit of his Son into our hearts" (Galatians 4:10; 2:20; 4:6).

73

The general teaching of all these passages is clear. The spirit in the inner man, Christ dwelling in our hearts, the spirit of God's Son in our hearts, Christ being formed in us—these all describe the result of that transformation "by the renewing of your mind" to which Paul exhorts the Romans (12:2). All comes about through the faith of the believer: Christ dwells in us "through faith"; the life Paul lives is "in faith".

But how much is implied by this! For here is not an unthinking or naive faith: it is based on an understanding of the truths of God: that is, His righteous judgement of human flesh because of sin; His manifestation of His own Spirit in the person of His Son; the conquest of sin and the atonement wrought by Christ; His gracious gift of righteousness to the enlightened and repentant sinner; the provision of those "words which are spirit and life", by which the humbled worshipper is enabled to understand the Spirit of God. All this is implied in "the faith in the Son of God" (Galatians 2:20). The Word of God exists to give us the necessary understanding of these saving truths. To imagine that we can dispense with it, that we can attain to communion with God without it, is to deliver ourselves up to the imaginings of the human mind, whether our own or another's.

But why does Paul associate the idea of strength and power with "the spirit of the inner man"?

He repeats the thought in the next two verses:

*". . . to the end that ye, being rooted and grounded in love, may be **strong** to apprehend the love of Christ . . . "*

(3:17,18, R.V.)

What is the connection between "love" and "strength"? The answer is illuminating. It is found first in the revelation of God to the people of Israel, who received the explicit command to act in mercy towards the poor, the fatherless and the widows among them. They were to leave the corners of their fields unreaped, and some fruit in the vineyards and the olive groves, so that the poor could glean them and find food to live.

In other ways, too, they were to act in mercy and compassion to the needy (see full details in Leviticus 19). No explicit reason is given, except the solemn reminder: "I am the Lord". But in Deuteronomy the reason is spelled out:

*"Thou shalt remember that thou wast a bondman in Egypt, and the Lord thy God redeemed thee thence:* **therefore** *I command thee to do this thing."* (24:18)

The divine reasoning is clear: the Israelites had been helpless slaves in Egypt, unable to save themselves. In His great mercy God had delivered them by His power. Because he had received this great demonstration of mercy from God, each individual Israelite was to act in a similar spirit towards his fellows. In saying "I am the LORD", God was reminding them of His own character of grace. The attitude of the Israelite to his fellows, in fact one of love, was based upon his realisation of his own redemption.

Of course the attitude of the believer in Christ is based upon the same principle:

*"Let all bitterness ... wrath ... anger ... clamour ... evil speaking, be put away from you, with all malice: and be ye kind one to another, tender-hearted, forgiving one another,* **even as God for Christ's sake hath forgiven you.***"* (Ephesians 4:31-32)

Here is the source of "strength": the man or woman who fully accepts his natural unworthiness in the sight of God, will be filled with thanksgiving for God's grace in his redemption. Fortified with this understanding, he will be far better able to carry out the demanding tasks of his calling. This, then, is why Paul says that if the Ephesians are "rooted and grounded in love", they will be "strong". This is not a strength introduced from outside themselves. It arises in their own minds from their understanding and acceptance of the revealed grace of God in their condition of need. It is a good illustration of the principle that the revealed truths of Scripture, when heartily understood and accepted, are powerful to influence the character. They call forth the willing cooperation of him who believes, and so contribute to that process of "renewing" and "transformation" so essential for salvation.

### "Filled with all the fulness of God"

We return to Ephesians chapter 3. Paul then prays that, having understood the greatness of the love of Christ (here, Christ's love for them), they may be "filled unto all the fulness of God" (verse 19).

What is this "fulness"? Again Christ is our example. Exhorting the Philippians to "lowliness of mind", Paul says:

> *"Have this mind in you, which was also in Christ Jesus, who ...* **emptied himself** *... humbled himself, becoming obedient even unto death."* (Philippians 2:5-8, R.V.).

Of what did Jesus "empty himself"? No doubt, firstly, of all claims to honour and glory from his fellow men, for he was after all the greatest man who ever walked this earth; he alone was "the only begotten Son of God". But then, equally, of all the natural pressures to fulfil his own desires, to develop "the mind of the flesh" and to manifest "the spirit of the world". Being thus emptied, he was in a position to be "filled" anew, now with the Spirit of God. So, says John, "we beheld his glory ... *full* of grace and truth" (John 1:14). "In Christ", writes Paul to the Colossians, "dwelleth all the fulness of the Godhead bodily". He then adds, "in whom ye are made full", and proceeds to tell them how: by being circumcised "in the putting off of the body of the flesh, in the circumcision of Christ" (2:9-11, R.V.), that is, of course, the circumcision of the heart.

In Ephesians 4 Paul explains how this "fulness" is attained by the community of believers. God has given apostles, prophets, evangelists, pastors and teachers,

> *"for the perfecting of the saints, unto the work of ministering, unto the building up of the body of Christ: till we all attain unto the unity of the faith, and of the knowledge of the Son of God, unto a fullgrown man, unto the measure of the stature of the **fulness** of Christ ... "* (verses 11-13, R.V.)

The "full grown man" is the new man in Christ. The "stature" of Christ is his spiritual maturity, his manifestation of the fulness of the Spirit of the Father. Of his "fulness" the saints also must partake. This is how they are to be filled with "the fulness of God" (Ephesians 3:19); not primarily an emotional or mystical experience, but a response to an understanding of the Spirit of God, a manifestation of its quality, based upon the instruction of His Word. As appreciation grows, it will bring its own emotional overtones of thankfulness and devotion. This is the "power that worketh in us".

76

The Apostle Paul has a number of other allusions to "power" and "working". To the Thessalonians he writes:

*"When ye received from us the word of the message, even the word of God, ye **accepted** it not as the word of men, but, as it is in truth, the **word of God**, which also **worketh** in you that believe."*

(1 Thessalonians 2:13)

If the Word of God works in the saints, then it is God who works. As Paul writes to the Philippians:

*". . . work out your own salvation with fear and trembling* (that is, in reverent worship)*; for it is God which worketh in you . . ."*

(Philippians 2:12-13)

—by your adopting the same "mind which was also in Christ Jesus."

Here is a valuable passage in Colossians. Paul prays,

*"that ye may be filled with the knowledge of (God's) will in all spiritual wisdom and understanding."*

This is a significant statement: it shows us what we ought to desire to be *filled* with: knowledge of the will of God, spiritual wisdom and understanding. The result will be:

*"to walk worthily of the Lord unto all pleasing, bearing fruit in every good work."*

That is, it will be shown in the believer's life. But the process does not come to a halt:

*"increasing in the knowledge of God",*

—not just the accumulation of information, but the continuing growth in wisdom, understanding, and appreciation of God. The result, says Paul, is that you will be

*"strengthened in (en) all power, according to the might of (God's) glory."*

This enables the committed believer to live in

*"all patience (endurance) and longsuffering with joy."*

(Colossians 1:9-11, R.V.)

Here the "strength" and the "power" are not injected from an external source into the believer. They develop in his mind as a result of his "increase in the knowledge of God" and of his appreciation of the true nature of God's "glory", His spiritual character.

77

All these passages, taken together, expound the great truth that the Word of God makes accessible His spiritual glory in the knowledge of Christ. That Word, when received with humility and faith, can counter the "power of Satan", the pressure of natural desires, for it has a power of its own: "the gospel, the power of God unto salvation". For this reason, Paul says again, the believers have not received from God "a spirit of fearfulness; but of *power* and love and discipline" (2 Timothy 1:7). This "spirit of power" arises from their understanding and acceptance of the truth of God, their faith and the manifestation of His mind and Spirit in their hearts. It is in this sense that we should understand "the power that worketh in us" (Ephesians 3:20).

## "Strengthened in the grace"

It will be helpful to consider a few more passages where the saints are said to be strengthened:

> *"Be strengthened in the grace that is in Christ Jesus."*
> (2 Timothy 2:1, R.V.)

There is an important truth here. The "grace" begins with God, who forgives the sins of the repentant believer, who then reacts to this with "gratitude" (same word in Greek) towards God; and because of his sense of the grace he has received, he can show the same gracious attitude to others. So his understanding of the grace received in Christ becomes a source of strength for its manifestation to others. In this way the saints can "abound in grace".

> *"Be strong in the Lord and in the strength of his might."*
> (Ephesians 6:10, R.V.)

In the verses that follow Paul tells how this comes about:

> *"Put on . . . take up the whole armour of God."*
> (verses 11,13)

> *". . . having girded your loins with truth* (that is, the full knowledge and understanding of the revealed will of God) *. . . put on the breastplate of righteousness* (the assurance that God will receive repentant sinners into right relationship with Himself)."
> (verse 14)

*". . . having shod your feet with the **preparation** of the **gospel of peace**" (preparation* only here in the New Testament: it is "preparedness", "the readiness and alacrity which the gospel produces"—Grimm-Thayer). (verse 15)

*". . . the shield of **faith** . . . "* (verse 16)

*". . . the helmet of **salvation*** (the "righteousness" of verse 15) *. . . the **sword of the Spirit** which is the **word of God*** (like Jesus at his temptation)." (verse 17)

*". . . **praying** at all seasons in (the) Spirit (en pneumati) . . . **watching** . . . "* (verse 17)

Armour of God, truth, righteousness, gospel of peace, faith, salvation, Word of God, prayer and watching: that is how we can be "strong in the Lord and in the strength of his might".

Peter has another interesting example in his First Epistle:

*"Blessed be God . . . who begat us again unto a living hope . . . unto an inheritance incorruptible . . . reserved in heaven for you, who by (the) **power of God** are **guarded** through **faith** unto a salvation ready to be revealed in the last time."* (1 Peter 1:3-5, R.V.)

What is this "power of God"? Three points must be noted. First, Peter wrote *en dunamei Theou, in* God-power (no article). He means "divine power", not human.

Second, the verb "guarded" is rare in the New Testament. It is a military term for guarding a camp etc.

Thirdly, this divine power operates "through faith", literally "by means of faith". We are inevitably reminded of Paul's saying, "that Christ may dwell in your hearts *through faith*". It looks as though this "power-of-God" is closely related to "Christ in your hearts". This is confirmed by Paul's use of the same verb "guarded" in Philippians:

*"In everything by prayer and supplication with thanksgiving let your requests be made known unto God. And the **peace of God** which passeth all understanding, shall **guard** your hearts and your thoughts in Christ Jesus."* (4:6-7, R.V.)

Again it is the rare word "guard". Notice it is "the peace of God" which guards—not just a tranquil mind, but that sense of reconciliation with God through the consciousness of sins forgiven

79

by faith in the sacrifice of Christ. This "peace" is a power in the believer's life, and as long as it prevails with thanksgiving, it will guard him in faithfulness. Once again the "power of God" is seen to arise from a real appreciation of what He has revealed in His Word.

The following extract sums up very well the theme of this section:

"The ideas and thoughts of the Deity are as much Spirit as His physical power. His thoughts are moral power *breathed forth* in His words, and that is Spirit ... His thoughts breathed forth, or revealed in any way He may determine, constitute 'the truth', and therefore the truth is Spirit. Hence the Lord Jesus said, 'My words are Spirit'; and the apostle John says, 'The Spirit is the truth'. To produce physical results, such as raising the dead, curing the sick, speaking with tongues, speaking by inspiration, material power or spirit is required; but when purely moral results are the things desired, the truth is the Spirit that operates upon the heart."

This was written over a hundred years ago in an article entitled "The Spirit of God and the Baptism Thereof" by John Thomas, reproduced in *The Christadelphian* 1875, page 487.

# 8

# "SPIRIT" AND "HOLY SPIRIT"

THERE are a number of allusions in the writings of the apostles to the Spirit and the Holy Spirit. As many of them are easy to quote, and equally easy to misapply, it is necessary to give careful attention to their context, and to the exact terms used.

We begin with a few passages where "the Spirit" as describing the "spiritual quality" of the mind of God (as distinct from the mind of the flesh) is called the "Holy Spirit".

Paul describes the attitude and experiences of himself and his fellow workers as

> *"ministers of God ... in afflictions ... in distresses ... by pureness, by knowledge, by longsuffering, by kindness, by (the) Holy Spirit, by love unfeigned, by (the) word of truth, by (the) power of God; by the armour of righteousness on the right hand and on the left ...*                    (2 Corinthians 6:4-7)

## "In Holy Spirit"

In this remarkable passage Paul uses the preposition *en* (in) no less than 18 times. The A.V. suitably renders it at first as "in": "in patience, in afflictions" etc., no less than 10 times; but then it switches to "by": "by the Holy Spirit" etc., 8 times. The R.V. corrects this inconsistency and has "in" throughout.

So "by the Holy Spirit" is really *en pneumati Theou*, "*in* Holy Spirit" (note the omission of the article). Now from a careful review of the context it seems unlikely that Paul was referring here to the miraculous powers of the Holy Spirit (though the New English Bible would have us think so by offering a paraphrase, "by gifts of the Holy Spirit", when there is no mention of "gifts" in the original). This is what Paul writes immediately before and after the term "Holy Spirit":

81

> *"... in pureness, in knowledge, in longsuffering, in kindness, in*
> **Holy Spirit,** *in love unfeigned, in word-of-truth, in power-of-God*
> *(en dunamei Theou), through the armour of righteousness ... "*

Here "Holy Spirit" is found amongst the spiritual qualities of pureness, longsuffering, kindness and love. Surely it must be of the same kind; that is, it signifies "the mind of the Spirit". So the "power-of-God", or divine power, is that exerted through the knowledge of the word of truth (see pages 70-72 for a treatment of this theme in Ephesians 3). Notice too that it is followed by "through the armour of righteousness". We are reminded of Paul's, "Be strong in the Lord and in the strength of his might. Put on the whole armour of God ..." (see page 78).

Here is another similar case:

> *"For the kingdom of God is not eating and drinking, but*
> *righteousness, peace and joy in (the) Holy Spirit" (en pneumati*
> *Theou).* (Romans 14:17)

To grasp the apostle's meaning, we need to appreciate that the word "kingdom" *(basileia)* in the New Testament has a wide sense, since it conveys both the authority of the King, and the area of his influence. So by "the kingdom of God" here, Paul means not the political kingdom to come, but the saints' preparation for that day by their yielding to the present dominion of God over them through the power of His Word. They are, even now, "delivered from the power of darkness, and translated into the kingdom of his dear Son" (Colossians 1:13). This membership of God's kingdom cannot be attained by rigid adherence to laws of food and drink (which some in Corinth wished to impose on their brethren). It exists in "righteousness, peace and joy in Holy Spirit". Clearly Holy Spirit here is the spiritual mind in which peace and joy can thrive. That it is a question of the *present* service of the believer, is shown by what follows:

> *"For he that herein serveth Christ ... "*

> *"Now the God of hope fill you with all joy and peace in believing,*
> *that ye may abound in hope, in (the) power of (the) Holy Spirit"*
> *(en dunamei pneumatos hagion*—no articles). (Romans 15:13)

## "Holy Spirit power"

The effect of the omission of the articles from the last phrase is to convey the sense: "Holy Spirit power". How are we to understand this? Earlier in the same chapter Paul had written:

> "For whatsoever things were written aforetime were written for our learning (our instruction, R.S.V.), that we through patience (steadfastness, R.S.V.) and comfort of the scriptures might have hope. Now the God of patience and consolation grant you to be like-minded . . . "  (verses 4,5)

The hope and the comfort (or encouragement, R.S.V.) come from a whole-hearted reception of the Scriptures. In this way God induces patience and comfort in His people. In the same way He is "the God of hope" (verse 13), because His revealed Word offers hope of salvation in place of death. The "joy" and "peace" come from "believing" this same revelation. "Holy Spirit power" arises as the Word of God renews and transforms by creating the mind of the Spirit, in place of the mind devoted to the flesh; the Word has spiritual power.

The context suggests that here again "Holy Spirit" represents not the miraculous power, but the mind or Spirit of God, conveyed to His saints through His Word, and powerful in "them that believe" (1 Thessalonians 2:13).

> "God . . . giveth his Holy Spirit unto you."
> (1 Thessalonians 4:8, R.V.)

## The Mind of the Spirit

Once again a careful study of the context makes Paul's meaning clear. The whole passage (verses 3-8) is an exhortation to sanctification:

> "For this is the will of God, even your sanctification, that ye should abstain from fornication: that every one of you should know how to possess his vessel (learn to control his own body, N.I.V.) in sanctification and honour . . . "  (verses 3-4)

> "God hath not called us unto uncleanness, but unto holiness . . . "
> (verse 7)

Paul's comments to the Corinthians on the same subject are helpful. In an exhortation to "flee fornication", he writes:

*"Know ye not that he which is joined to an harlot is one body . . .?*
*But he that is joined unto the Lord is* **one spirit** *. . ."*

(1 Corinthians 6:16)

That is, he shares with the Lord one mind, or one spirit. Paul
then adds:

*"He that committeth fornication sinneth against his own body"*

because the body is the means through which the "one spirit"
should be manifested. This is now what he proceeds to say:

*"Know ye not that your body is* **a** *(R.V.) temple of (the) Holy Spirit*
*which is in you, which ye have of God?"*

The "one spirit" with the Lord, and "Holy Spirit" (no article
again) manifested in the body are evidently the same thing.
"Holy Spirit" in the believer is "God-Spirit" or "Christ-Spirit"
in him, as Paul expounds in Romans 8 (see pages 54-58). This is
"his Holy Spirit" which "God gives unto us" as we adopt the
way of "sanctification". Note the great contrast between "the
Spirit" which is "holy" and the uncleanness of fornication.

The few passages just considered show that the "mind of the
spirit" is described not only as "Spirit" but also as "Holy
Spirit". To imagine, as some do, that the Holy Spirit must
always imply miraculous powers, or, as others do, some direct action by the Holy Spirit on the mind (is not that only a refinement
of the miraculous gift?) is to mistake the meaning of Scripture.
"Holy Spirit" is used to describe the spiritual quality of the mind
of God, whether manifested by the Lord God Himself or in His
faithful servants. As Jesus put it, "God is Spirit", and He must
be worshipped "in spirit and in truth" (John 4:23).

### The "Letter" and "the Spirit"

In 2 Corinthians 3 the Apostle Paul has a very helpful passage on
the work of the Spirit:

*" . . . ye are an epistle of Christ, ministered by us, written not with*
*ink, but with (the) Spirit of (the) living God; not in tables of stone,*
*but in tables that are hearts of flesh."*

(2 Corinthians 3:3, R.V.)

The Corinthians had believed the gospel of Christ which Paul
had preached to them. As a result, their hearts had been "written
upon" by the message they had received, and the writing had

84

been done by "living God-Spirit" *(pneumati Theou zōntas)*—note the absence of articles. How does this Spirit work in the hearts and minds of those who believe? There are two passages in Proverbs which Paul must have had in mind:

> *"Let not mercy and truth forsake thee . . . write them upon the table of thine heart."* (Proverbs 3:3)

> *"My son, keep my words . . . Keep my commandments, and live; and my law as the apple of thine eye . . . Write them upon the table of thine heart. Say unto wisdom, Thou art my sister; and call understanding thy kinswoman . . . "* (Proverbs 7:1-4)

Here the writer is commending "mercy and truth" (two key terms which summarise God's revelation of Himself to Israel); and "the words, the commandments, the law", the detailed means by which this divine revelation was to be understood. The result will be "written on the heart" and its nature is described as "wisdom" and "understanding". Clearly, once again, "heart" is being used for "mind". When it is "renewed unto knowledge" (Colossians 3:10) the enlightened mind manifests "living God-Spirit", or "Christ-Spirit" (see section on Romans 8, pages 54-58).

Paul refers to this process in what he goes on to say in 2 Corinthians 3. He contrasts the Law and the Gospel as two "ministrations", or covenants (see verse 6): one "of letter", "of death", and "of condemnation"; and the other "of spirit" and "of righteousness". Israel, by their rejection of Christ, had preferred "the letter" to "the spirit", and would remain unenlightened until they "turned to the Lord". The apostle then concludes:

> *"Now the Lord is the Spirit: and where the Spirit of the Lord is, there is liberty. But we all with open face reflecting (beholding, A.V.) as a mirror the glory of the Lord, are transformed into the same image from glory to glory, even as from the Lord the Spirit."* (verses 17-18, R.V.)

## The Process of Transformation

In this remarkable passage Paul equates the Spirit with Christ, and shows what he means by describing it as "the Spirit of the Lord" (or as he had written in Romans 8, "the Spirit of Christ").

The devoted followers "behold" the glory of the Lord; that is, they "set their mind on" Christ, with no casual glance, but with a purposive contemplation. They are beholding Christ as "the image" of God, the manifestation of the Divine mind. This is Christ's spiritual glory. As they contemplate him, Paul appears to say by a second sense of the same verb, they come to "reflect" as a mirror does, the spiritual image of Christ; and so they are "transformed, from glory into glory" *(apo doxēs eis doxan).*

Conybeare and Howson have an interesting comment on this verse. They translate: "We all, while with face unveiled we behold in a mirror the glory of the Lord, are ourselves *transformed continually* into the same likeness; and the glory which shines upon us is reflected by us, even as it proceeds from the Lord, the Spirit". They add this note: "'From glory' indicates the origin of this transformation, viz. the glory shining upon us; 'to glory', the effect: viz. the reflection of that glory by us". *(Life and Letters of St. Paul,* page 446).

The general tenor of this chapter is the power of the new "ministration", the new covenant, to transform the minds and hearts of believers, by assuring them of "righteousness" (that is, their right relationship with God through their belief of the gospel, repentance and faith, and the forgiveness of their sins); and then by presenting Christ as the manifestation of the Spirit of God in his words, his works, and his ways. As the saints "set their mind on" his spiritual image, and develop the same spirit themselves, they also partake of the divine spiritual glory.

It is clear that the work of the Spirit here is not one of sudden illumination from an external source. It is a process of transformation of heart and mind, as a result of the preaching of Paul and his fellow workers. It results from knowledge and understanding, culminating in wisdom (compare his prayer for the Colossians: "that ye may be filled with . . . all spiritual wisdom and understanding" (1:9), so that the faithful come to reflect in themselves something of the spiritual glory of Christ. The process remains exactly the same today. The means available to us are the same as those enjoyed by the Corinthians. They had the words of Paul; we have them too, but written down in the Word of God, together with "many like words". If heartily received, they are the source for us of "spirit and life", as Jesus said of his own sayings (John 6:63).

### The Use of *ek* (out of)

We consider next two passages from the Apostle John:

> *"Hereby we know that he (Christ) abideth in us, by the Spirit which he hath given us."* (1 John 3:24)

> *"Hereby know we that we dwell in him (God), and he in us, because he hath given us of his Spirit."* (1 John 4:13)

In what sense is John using "Spirit" here? It will help to note exactly what he wrote. Twice he has used the preposition *ek*, usually translated "of" or "from", but basically meaning "out of". So

> *". . . by (ek, out of) the Spirit which he gave us."*

> *". . . he hath given us of (ek, out of) his Spirit."*

Here are further examples of the use of *ek* from John's Gospel:

> The *"sons of God"* are those born, *"not of (ek) blood, nor of (ek) the will of the flesh, nor of (ek) the will of man, but of (ek) God."*
> (1:13)

Here *ek* conveys the idea that the children not only owe their origin to God, but being *ek*, out of, Him, they possess His very nature: that is, His spiritual nature. Since they all share a nature of flesh and blood, the reference is to the spirit of their minds. Those who are of (*ek*) the flesh and of (*ek*) man, do the will of the flesh; those who are of (*ek*) God, do the will of God.

So Jesus could say of the Jews:

> *"Ye are from (ek) beneath . . . of (ek) this world . . . of (ek) the devil."*

Of himself Jesus said:

> *"I am from (ek) above . . . I came forth and am come from (ek) God."* (John 8:23,42,44)

Here are the two wisdoms described by James: one from the earth, earthy; the other, from above (3:15-17).

In John's First Epistle (from which the two quotations at the head of this section are taken) the expression is frequent. The saints are not "of (*ek*) the world", nor "of (*ek*) the devil", but "of (*ek*) God" (2:16; 3:8,19; 4:4 etc.). So when he says that God has given us "of (*ek*) his Spirit", we recognise his idiom. He means that, as devoted servants, we partake not of the spirit of the world and the flesh, but of the Spirit of God; we share His mind, embrace His will, and seek to walk in His ways. We know the difference between "the spirit of truth and the spirit of error" (3:6).

In each of the two quotations at the head of this section John says, "we *know* ...", because of the Spirit. It is helpful to note the various signs by which the saints may "know". Here are examples:

> *"We* **know** *that we have passed out of (ek) death into life* **because we love the brethren."** (1 John 3:14)

> *"We do* **know** *that we know him,* **if we keep his command-ments."** (2:3)

> *"Let us not* **love** *in word, neither in tongue, but in deed and in truth ... and hereby we* **know** *that we are of (ek)* **the truth."** (3:18-19)

> *"We are of (ek) God ... we* **know** *the spirit of truth, and the spirit of error."* (4:6)

> *"Love is of (ek) God ... every one that loveth is born of God, and* **knoweth God."** (4:7)

> *"We know that the Son of God ... hath given us* **an under-standing,** *that we may* **know** *him that is true ... are* **in** *him ... even in his Son Jesus ... This is ... eternal life."* (5:20)

These passages are all saying the same thing: the saints *know* that there is a different spirit in them than there is in the world, because they have an understanding; they know (in the fullest sense) the truth, they keep the commandments, they love the brethren, they are begotten of God. "The Spirit which God hath given us" is the fruit of this understanding and knowledge of the truth. Again it is "the mind of the Spirit."

## Sanctification of Spirit

Two passages are of particular interest, since they are often quoted by those who believe that the servants of Christ need to be "sanctified" by some direct action of the Holy Spirit.

> *"God hath from the beginning chosen you to salvation through* (R.V., *in*) *sanctification of the Spirit and belief of the truth."* (2 Thessalonians 2:13)

Close attention to what Paul actually wrote is important here: "in sanctification of spirit and belief of truth" *(en hagiasmō pneumatos kai pistei alētheias)*. Note the total absence of the definite articles. Note also that it is "in *(en)* sanctification of spirit", a state rather than an action.

The natural way to read Paul's words is as two parallel expressions: as truth is believed, so spirit is sanctified; the sanctification is of the believer's spirit which accompanies his belief of the truth. This understanding of Paul's words is admitted by some commentators: "The omission of the article in the Greek is difficult to explain if the 'spirit' mentioned by other than the spirit acted upon" (Ellicott, *Commentary*); "By the consecration of your spirit" (Moffatt); "Understood by some . . . of the sanctification of the believer's spirit" (Leon Morris, "Thessalonians", *New International Commentary*)—though in the end theological bias prevails and most commentators reject this interpretation because it does not support "the activity of the Spirit". Of course the origin of this sanctification is in the Holy Spirit of God, but it is mediated, says Paul, by "belief of truth" (that is, the truth revealed in the Word of God), and it is manifested in the believer's own spirit.

The identical expression is found in Peter:

*". . . elect according to the foreknowledge of God the Father, through sanctification of (the) spirit (en hagiasmō pneumatos, no article) unto obedience and sprinkling of the blood of Jesus Christ."*

(1 Peter 1:2)

The reference to God the Father and to Jesus encourages commentators to claim a trinitarian reference here for "Spirit". But the claim is purely a matter of interpretation. The Speaker's *Commentary* is frank: "The expression is not without ambiguity, as it may mean sanctification of the Spirit, bestowed by the Holy Ghost, or sanctification of the believer's spirit." Schonfield, the Jewish scholar, who was not hampered by trinitarian theology, translates the two passages thus: "consecration of spirit and attachment to truth" (Thessalonians); "by spiritual consecration" (Peter). Again, it is difficult to resist the conclusion that if Peter had meant the sanctifying *act* of the Holy Spirit on the believer's mind, he would have written "sanctification of *the*

Spirit", and he would probably not have used the preposition *en*, in.*

## The Fellowship of the Spirit

> *"The grace of the Lord Jesus Christ, and the love of God, and the communion of the Holy Spirit, be with you all."*
>
> (2 Corinthians 13:14)

The word communion *(koinōnia)* means a common sharing in, a fellowship. Since the grace proceeds from Christ, and the love from God, one would expect the fellowship to proceed from the Holy Spirit. We shall see that this is true, although the proper sense of the expression needs to be understood.

The Apostle Paul has a helpful parallel in his letter to Philippi:

> *"If there is therefore any comfort in Christ, if any consolation of love, if any fellowship of (the) Spirit, if any tender mercies and compassions . . ."* (Philippians 2:1, R.V.)

This time the apostle wrote "fellowship of spirit" *(koinōnia pneumatos*, no article). The "spirit" is of the same kind as the love, the mercy and the compassion: that is, it is an experience of the mind, the manifestation in the believers of God's Spirit, instead of the spirit of their own desires. This "mind of the spirit" they share in common. Paul's "fellowship of the Holy Spirit" means substantially the same thing, for it is that special quality of the mind of God which is the Holy Spirit in its "spiritual" sense (not its miraculous). When John writes, "our fellowship *(koinōnia*, communion, same word) is with the Father and the Son" (1 John 1:3), he means that the saints share with God and with Christ the same understanding of truth, the same spiritual outlook. This is Paul's "fellowship of the Holy Spirit". In 2 Corinthians 13:14 the article is retained in "the Holy Spirit" because Paul, having just mentioned grace and love from Christ and God, is thinking of the same origin of this "Holy Spirit": it originates with God Himself, and is mediated to His people through His Word of truth. The article is omitted in Philippians because Paul is thinking not now of its origin but of its manifestation in the saints.

---

*There is a helpful article on "In Sanctification of the Spirit" by W. L. Bedwell in *The Christadelphian*, 1957, page 52.

## Renewing of Holy Spirit

*". . . according to his mercy (God) saved us, by (the) washing of regeneration, and renewing of (the) Holy Spirit* (remarkably no articles at all). *"* (Titus 3:5-6)

What does Paul mean by "renewing of Holy Spirit"? He goes on to say, "which he poured upon us richly", using the aorist tense, thus conveying the impression that it was a decisive act, not a continuous process. This has led some to think that he is referring to the pouring out of the power of the Holy Spirit at Pentecost. But since he says it was by this that God "saved us . . . through Jesus Christ our Saviour, (we) being justified by his grace", it is much more likely to be a reference to the manifestation of God's Spirit in Christ, in which sin was conquered, atonement was made, and redemption made possible through the belief of the gospel, that "power of God unto salvation".

Two further allusions confirm this. One is the association of "washing" in other Scriptures:

*"Born of* **water** *and of the Spirit . . . "* (John 3:5)

*". . .* **washed** *us from our sins in his own blood . . . "*
(Revelation 1:5)

*". . .* **washed** *. . . sanctified . . . justified in the name of (the Lord Jesus). "* (1 Corinthians 6:11)

*"Christ . . . having cleansed (the ecclesia) by the* **washing** *of water* **with the word**. *"* (Ephesians 5:26, R.V.)

This last quotation is interesting, for it tells us how the cleansing and washing are accomplished: "with the word". But Paul uses *rhēma* for "word", that is, "a saying", and of course the teaching conveyed by it. Three times in Romans 10 he uses *rhēma* for the preaching of the gospel:

*"The word (rhēma) is nigh thee . . . the word (rhēma) of faith which we preach . . . Faith cometh by hearing, and hearing by the word (rhēma) of Christ. "* (verses 8,17)

The reception of this word in faith leads to "new birth" (regeneration). The believer is "born again . . . of water and spirit". He is a "new creature".

91

The second allusion is in the use of "renewing" in other New Testament passages:

*". . . our inward man is renewed . . . "* (2 Corinthians 4:16)

*". . . transformed by the renewing of your mind. "*

(Romans 12:2)

*". . . the new man . . . renewed unto knowledge . . . after the image of (God). "* (Colossians 3:10, R.V.)

*"Be renewed in the spirit of your mind. "* (Ephesians 4:23)

Paul's "renewing" of (the) Holy Spirit" must refer to the same process. It is that new birth in the believer whereby he repudiates the mind of the flesh and seeks to develop the mind of the spirit. This is confirmed by what he writes in his second chapter:

> *"Christ . . . gave himself for us, that he might redeem us from all iniquity, and **purify unto himself** a people for his own possession"* (Titus 2:13,14, R.V.)

The "purifying" proceeds by "washing" and "renewing".

Paul's phrase, "through renewing of (the) Holy Spirit, which (God) poured out upon us", finds a parallel in his saying to the Romans:

> *". . . the **love of God** hath been shed abroad in our hearts through (the) Holy Spirit which was given unto us. "*

(Romans 5:5, R.V.)

Vine says that "shed abroad" is a closely related verb to "poured out" in Titus 3:6. The love of God can only be abundantly manifested in the hearts and minds of those who *understand what it means*, who appreciate and respond to it. This is how the Spirit of God works in the faithful—through understanding and response.

## "The Comforter" Passages in John

John's Gospel records that Jesus, in his last talk with his disciples before his crucifixion, told them he was soon going away, but promised that they would not be left "orphans". "I will pray the Father", he said, "and he shall give you another Comforter" (14:16). In John's Gospel he returns to the subject at verse 26, and in 15:26-27 and 16:7-14. Apart from the application of the term to Jesus in John's First Epistle (2:1), where it is translated "advocate", these are its only Scriptural occurrences.

Two preliminary points can usefully be made, before we come to look at the passages in detail. The first is that "Comforter" is not a satisfactory rendering of the term *paraklētos*, which means one who comes to the help of another. 'Advocate', 'Helper' and 'Friend' have all been favoured by various students of the Greek. The second is that by their translations modern theologians unitedly suggest that the Advocate is to be regarded as a person, by consistently using "he" and "him". But in the passages listed above, the pronoun is sometimes masculine, referring to the masculine noun *paraklētos*, and sometimes neuter, referring to the neuter noun *pneuma* (spirit). While some maintain that the use of the term Advocate is a personification, there would appear to be no strictly grammatical evidence that John was so using it.

A brief survey of the relevant passages produces the following:

The Advocate is "the Spirit of *the* truth", which will be sent by the Father in Jesus' name; it is the Holy Spirit, which will teach the disciples all things, and "bring all things to your remembrance, whatsoever I have said unto you" (14:16,26).

The Advocate is "the Spirit of the truth", which Jesus will send from the Father. It will "bear witness of me" to reinforce the witness of the disciples themselves (15:26-27).

The Advocate will only come if Jesus goes away. Called once more "the Spirit of *the* truth", it would guide the disciples into all *the* truth and would "declare unto you the things that are to come" (16:7-14).

It is evident that these promises of help for the apostles were fulfilled by the powers which were granted to them at Pentecost and afterwards. The apostles had a mighty aid in their witness that it was Jesus of Nazareth who was the promised Messiah, and that the work of God through him was for Israel's redemption and salvation. But the description "the Spirit of truth", used three times in these passages, deserves some exploration. Literally it is "the Spirit of *the* truth". Now "the truth" is the commonist Biblical term for the purpose of God for salvation. It was used in the Old Testament for God's covenant with Israel. It is used for the gospel: God desires all men to be saved, and "to come unto the *knowledge of the truth*" (1 Timothy 2:4). It is closely linked with the Word: "sanctify (the disciples) through thy truth: thy word is truth" (John 17:17). And Jesus himself was the very embodiment of it: "I am the truth", he told them (John 14:6).

This "Spirit of the truth" the "world cannot receive" (verse 17). That is what Paul writes about "the natural man", who "receiveth not the things of the Spirit of God" (1 Corinthians 2:14). Jesus goes on to say that, unlike the world which "knows not" this Spirit of the truth, the disciples *do* know it (him), and then adds:

> *"for it (he) abideth with you and shall be in you."*
> (John 14:17, R.V.)

Now these expressions inevitably recall other sayings in the New Testament. Shortly Jesus would say to his disciples:

> *"If ye abide in me, and my words abide in you ..."*
> (15:7)

He had earlier said:

> *"If ye abide in my word, then are ye truly my disciples, and ye shall know the truth ..."*  (8:31,32, R.V.)

The idea of Christ dwelling in the disciples by their understanding of his mind and their reflection of it in themselves is frequently found in the Epistles. Paul desired that Christ might be "formed" in the Galatians by their growing understanding of the truth. He prays for the Ephesians that "Christ may dwell in your hearts (minds) through faith" (3:17). To the Colossians this becomes: "Let the word of Christ dwell in you richly in all *wisdom*" (3:16); and shortened still further: "*Christ in you*, the hope of glory" (1:27).

Now this is what Jesus proceeds to say in his further comments to the disciples in John 14. It is best to take them all together. When he was raised from the dead,

> *"in that day ye shall know that I am in the Father, and ye in me, and I in you. He that hath my commandments, and keepeth them, he it is that loveth me: and he that loveth me shall be loved of my Father, and I will love him, and will manifest myself unto him ... If a man love me, he will keep my word: and my Father will love him, and we will come unto him, and make our abode with him ..."*  (verses 20-23, R.V.)

94

In other words, if the disciples keep Christ's word, and his commandments, and love him, he and his Father will abide "with them" and "in them". There is a "unity of the Spirit" in them all, because they share the mind of the Spirit, that is, of God and of Christ (Romans 8).

The teaching of these "Comforter" passages, especially that of John 14:16-24, now becomes clearer. Jesus begins by promising the disciples an Advocate, a Helper, a Friend, which will assist them in their work of preaching. It is called "the Spirit of the truth" and "the Holy Spirit". It will powerfully reinforce their witness to him; it will aid their understanding of the things Jesus had already taught them. Notice the important fact that this gift of the Spirit would not reveal to them any new doctrine: it would make clear what Jesus had already said. It would reinforce the Spirit and the word of Christ. It would aid in convicting the world of sin, righteousness and judgement. It would "guide them into all *the* truth", and "declare things that are to come" (16:13).

But Jesus' description of this Helper as "the Spirit of the truth" leads him to contemplate the situation of his followers beyond the apostolic age, even "for ever" (14:16). Clearly the special powers did not last "for ever". But the spiritual understanding needed for salvation would grow in the ecclesias, and the means of absorbing it would be perpetuated in the apostolic writings, the God-breathed Word for successive generations. Right down to our own day it has been possible for earnest minds to understand and to manifest "the spirit of the truth".

Here once again we have both aspects of the Spirit of God: the powerful and the spiritual. We no longer have the special power; but we still have "the Comforter's word",* by which we may appreciate "the Spirit of the truth", and may receive the comforting assurance that God is with us and may be in us.

### "The promise of the Spirit"

The Apostle Paul's allegory of Ishmael and Isaac provides a valuable illustration of the "promise of the Spirit" (Galatians 3:14). From the record in Genesis of Abraham's two sons,

---

*For a more extended treatment of this theme, see the C.M.P.A. article, "The Work of the Holy Spirit", *The Christadelphian*, 1983, page 295.

Ishmael born of "the handmaid" Hagar, and Isaac born of "the freewoman" Sarah, the apostle deduces the birth of two seeds. The one he describes as "born according to the flesh" and the other "born through promise" (R.S.V.). The first represented those under "the covenant from Mount Sinai"; they were "in bondage" to the Law. But the second seed were children of the "Jerusalem which is above, which is our mother". Her children are "free", not under the bondage of the Law.

Turning to the believers in Christ, Paul says:

> *"Now we are the **children of promise** . . . "* (4:28)

He then enlarges his description of the two seeds:

> *"He that was born according to (the) flesh (kata sarka) . . . he that was born according to (the) Spirit (kata pneuma)."* (4:29)

Of course Isaac was born "through promise" and "according to Spirit" in a very remarkable way. He was the son of Abraham's faith in the promises, and he was born by direct intervention of the Spirit of God when his parents were beyond the age of child bearing. So, the apostle is saying to the believers in Christ, we are "children of promise . . . born according to Spirit". As Jesus said to Nicodemus, they are "born of water and of spirit" through their belief in the gospel. They are also "heirs of the promise" made to Abraham and his seed. What is interesting about Paul's use of these descriptions of the faithful is his association of "the promise" with "Spirit". So those who have faith in the promises of God and live in the spirit of His commandments are born of the wisdom that comes from above (James 3), of "the Jerusalem . . . above", and so "of Spirit".

> *" . . . that upon the Gentiles might come the blessing of Abraham in Christ Jesus; that we might receive **the promise of the Spirit** through faith."* (Galatians 3:14, R.V.)

Like a number of other expressions of similar form, "the promise of the Spirit" is ambiguous. It could mean "that which the Spirit has promised", or equally "the Spirit which has been promised". We need to examine the context very carefully to see what must have been in the apostle's mind. For this we must go back to the beginning of the chapter:

> *"Received ye the Spirit by (the) works of (the) law, or by (the) hearing of faith? Are ye so foolish? having begun in (the) Spirit, are ye now*

*perfected in (the) flesh? . . . He therefore that supplieth to you the*
*Spirit, and worketh miracles among you, doeth he it by (the) works*
*of (the) law, or by (the) hearing of faith?''*     (3:2-5, R.V.)

What is this "Spirit" which the Galatians had received and
God had "supplied"? At first sight the reference to "miracles"
(or "powers") appears to be to the Holy Spirit gift, but other
phrases suggest another emphasis. Paul says the Galatians have
"begun" and need to be "perfected". This is clearly a reference
to their life of faith and their spiritual growth in Christ. Further,
his question, "Having begun by-Spirit (*pneumati*, one word), can
you be perfected by-flesh (*sarki*, one word)", suggests that he is
referring to their understanding of the Spirit of God and of
Christ, not to an endowment with miraculous powers. So "he
that supplieth to you the Spirit and worketh miracles among you"
conveys the two aspects of the work of the Spirit: the enlightenment of the understanding, accompanied in the apostolic age by
miraculous powers as an aid to witness. Paul explains what he
means by "supplying the Spirit", in the next chapter:

*"Because ye are sons* (of God, by adoption, see verse 5), *God*
*hath sent forth the Spirit of his Son into your hearts, crying,*
*Abba, Father.''*     (4:6)

A little later he shows how he understands God's "sending
forth the Spirit of his Son into their hearts", by expressing his
dismay that it was not occurring in the Galatian believers as it
should:

*"My little children, of whom I am again in travail until Christ*
*be formed in you."*     (verse 19, R.V.)

This is clearly an allusion to the development in their minds (or
hearts) of the understanding of the Spirit of God and of Christ,
in contrast with the spirit of the flesh. As Paul wrote to the Corinthians: "that the *life* also *of Jesus* might be made manifested in our
mortal flesh" (2 Corinthians 4:11); or to the Philippians: "Let
this *mind* be in you, which was also in Christ Jesus . . ." (2:5).

This, then, is how God had "supplied the Spirit" to the
Galatian believers: "by (the) hearing of faith" (3:2), where, says
Vine, it is "the hearing of a *message*". In other words, to the
Galatians the Gospel had been preached, with the sound instruc-
tion of the Law and the Prophets.

It is with this background that in verse 14, "the blessing of Abraham" is associated with "the promise of the Spirit". In the remaining verses of this chapter the "promises to Abraham" are referred to no less than eight times: five times as "the promise", twice as "the promises", and once as "the inheritance". The passage concludes:

*"For as many of you as have been baptized into Christ have* **put on Christ** *... Ye are all one* **in Christ Jesus**. *And if ye be Christ's, then are ye Abraham's seed, and heirs according to the promise."*
(verses 27-29)

Notice the emphasis on the Gentile believers' being "in Christ" and "putting on Christ". This last expression is explained in the following:

*"Put ye on the Lord Jesus Christ, and make not provision for the flesh."* (Romans 13:14)

*"Be renewed in the spirit of your mind, and ... put on the new man ..."* (Ephesians 4:23)

*"Put on the new man, which is being renewed unto knowledge, after the (spiritual) image of (God) ..."* (Colossians 3:10, R.V.)

So Paul's argument to the Galatians is: if you "put on Christ" in developing the mind of Christ (which of course cannot be done without understanding and faith), then you qualify as Abraham's seed and become heirs of the promise. We should notice that he does *not* say: 'If you believe the promises made to Abraham, you are automatically in Christ'. The priority is to be "in Christ", to have "put on Christ", for it would be quite possible to believe the promises to Abraham and yet to manifest an unChristlike spirit.

Now to be "in Christ" in this sense is to manifest the Spirit of Christ in mind and heart. The conclusion from Paul's exposition must be that the essence of the promises to Abraham was not just that the faithful will inherit the land of promise, though they certainly will, but even more that in his seed (which is Christ) would "all nations of the earth be blessed"; blessed, that is, with life instead of death, with the mind of the Spirit instead of the mind of flesh. This is "the promise of the Spirit through faith". It is the same as "the promise of the life which is in Christ Jesus"

(2 Timothy 1:1). It is also in John's mind as he writes his First Epistle:

> *"If that which ye heard from the beginning* **abide** *in you, ye also shall* **abide in the Son** *and* **in the Father.** *And this is the* **promise** *which he promised us, even the* **life eternal.**"
>
> (1 John 2:24-25)

(For the passages in John on "abiding" and "eternal life", see Chapter 9.)

### "The gift of the Holy Spirit"

> *"Repent ye, and be baptized every one of you in the name of Jesus Christ unto the remission of your sins; and ye shall receive the gift of the Holy Spirit. For to you is the promise, and to your children, and to all that are afar off, even as many as the Lord our God shall call unto him."* (Acts 2:36-38, R.V.)

This much discussed passage is based upon the prophecy of Joel, quoted extensively by Peter in verses 17-21. That quotation makes these points:

1. The prophecy applies to the last days (verse 17).
2. The pouring out of God's Spirit will result in "prophesying" by those from all parts of Israel's society. "To prophesy" means to speak forth the Word of God by the power of divine inspiration. It is important to notice that the promise does *not* concern miracles, but prophesying.
3. At the same period there are to be great signs in the heaven and in the earth, "blood, fire, and smoke". It will be "the great and terrible day of the Lord" (verse 20).
4. Whoever calls on the name of the Lord will be saved (verse 20).

It is clear that Peter and his fellow apostles saw the Holy Spirit gift of tongues which they had just received as in some way a fulfilment of Joel's prophecy. Whether Peter thought the "wonders" and fearful events would soon follow we have no means of knowing. In the event, the outpouring of the Spirit upon the apostles was an "earnest" or guarantee of that greater outpouring to come in the last days.

Peter's address to those present in Jerusalem is an excellent example of "prophesying". It consists of an explanation of God's

Word through Jesus of Nazareth, who had first been "approved . . . by miracles, wonders and signs", and had finally been raised from the dead and had ascended to heaven, there to become "Lord and Christ". The urgent message was not to aspire to receive the miraculous gift but to "repent and be baptized . . . in the name of the Lord Jesus, for the remission of your sins". This message of redemption and salvation was addressed to "every one of you".

When Peter goes on to say, "Ye shall receive the gift of the Holy Spirit", his hearers must have understood him to mean the same sort of gift as he and his fellow apostles had just received— that indicated by Joel, the gift of prophesying. It is important to note that the gift was to be granted *after* their repentance and their baptism (which had not yet taken place). The gift of the Spirit would not cause their conversion. It would come afterwards as a witness to the truth of the Gospel they had believed.

What in fact happened? Peter's hearers "gladly received his word and were baptized", and "continued steadfastly in the apostles' teaching and fellowship . . . with one accord in the temple . . . praising God and having favour with all the people". But there is no mention of their receiving any striking gift of the Spirit. The "wonders and signs" were done by the apostles and not by the multitude (verse 43).

The remaining history of Acts describes three occasions of the gift of the Holy Spirit being granted. The first was to the believers in Samaria, who had accepted "the gospel of the kingdom and the name" preached by Philip, but only after the apostles had made a special journey from Jerusalem to confer it. Philip himself was evidently unable to do this (Acts 8). The second was to Cornelius and his household as a powerful witness for the benefit of Peter and his fellow Jews, that Gentile believers must unreservedly be received into the community (Acts 10). The third was to the followers of John the Baptist who, after their baptism into the name of the Lord Jesus, received the Holy Spirit by the laying on of Paul's hands, and as a result "spake with tongues and prophesied" (Acts 19). It is highly likely that all these gifts were of a temporary nature, meant to be a witness and an encouragement. The fact that only the apostles could pass them on to

100

others makes it certain that this manifestation of the Spirit must in time have ceased.

The promise then of a spectacular outpouring of the Spirit upon all believers was not fulfilled after Peter's preaching at Pentecost. But another promise was. Joel's prophecy of the outpouring of the Spirit concluded with the promise that "whosoever shall call on the name of the Lord shall be delivered: for in mount Zion and in Jerusalem shall be deliverance ... and in the remnant whom the LORD shall call" (2:32). Peter, with the sanction of the Holy Spirit interprets this thus:

*"Whosoever shall call on the name of the Lord shall be* **saved** ...
*The promise is unto you, and to your children, and to all that are afar off, even as many as the Lord our God shall call."*

(verses 21,39)

If Peter's saying is a comment on the conclusion of Joel's prophecy, which seems probable, the promise he means is that of salvation and deliverance for "those who call upon the name of the Lord"—the same that "the Lord shall call". Their deliverance was by the remission of their sins through their belief in and obedience to the Gospel. In this way they would be *saved* "from this crooked generation" (Acts 2:40, R.V.).

This is the understanding of Peter's words most consistent with the facts. There was a limited manifestation of the Spirit of "prophesying" in the days of the apostles—no doubt it will be far greater when "the great and terrible day of the LORD" finally comes. But there was an immediate and unconditional promise of "salvation" for all who repented and were baptized, a promise which extended to "those afar off". Peter's audience would no doubt understand this as applying to faithful Israelites living in distant parts of the Roman Empire. But Paul in Ephesians 2 makes it clear that the allusion was intended by the Spirit to be to the call of the Gentiles.

## "...the Holy Spirit to them that ask him"

*"If ye, being evil, know how to give good gifts unto your children, how much more shall your heavenly Father give (the) Holy Spirit to them that ask him?"*
(Luke 11:13)

"Holy Spirit" (without the article) is the regular description of the effect upon the believers in apostolic times when they had received the gift of the Holy Spirit (see chapter 5 for details). But is Jesus here promising special powers direct from God to "them that ask him"? The promise seems so wide in its scope, and the special powers were so limited in theirs, that it is unlikely that he was referring primarily to them. In the parallel passage in Matthew 7:7-11 the promise appears thus: "How much more shall your Father in heaven give *good things* to them that ask him?" What are these "good things" and what is their relation to "Holy Spirit"?

Other New Testament passages throw some light on the matter. In the previous chapter in Matthew the Lord tells the disciples what they are to "seek":

> *"Seek ye first the kingdom of God, and his righteousness; and all these things* (the needs of this natural life, see verses 31-32) *shall be added unto you."* (6:33)

Now the whole tenor of Jesus' words to them in Matthew 6:19-34 is an exhortation to faith and trust in God's control of their affairs for good. This is "the kingdom" they are to "seek" through His Word (see comments on Romans 14:17, page 82); and "his righteousness" is that "rightness" or reconciliation that He will extend to the repentant sinner.

Again, Jesus tells the woman of Samaria that if she had known "the gift of God" and who it was who was asking her for water, she would have asked of hi;. and he would have given her "living water". Jesus further describes this water: "Whoso drinketh of the water that I shall give him, (that water) shall *become in him* a well of water springing up unto *eternal life*" (John 4:10,14).

And a final clue: in Romans 15 the apostle Paul, referring to the preaching of the Gospel, exclaims: "How beautiful are the feet of them that bring glad tidings of *good things*" (verse 15). It is the same word *agatha* ('good', neuter plural) which Jesus had used in Matthew 7:11.

There is no doubt, then, what the "good things" are which God will give to those who ask Him. They are the good news of the gospel; the knowledge of Christ's teaching which works in the faithful like a well of water producing "eternal life" (see comments on "eternal life" in Chapter 9; and God's influence over him through obedience to His Word and His provision for all needs.

What then was mainly in Jesus' mind when he promised "Holy Spirit"? Clearly not miraculous powers, but rather "holy spirit", a "spirit of holiness" like that which commended Jesus himself to God (see Romans 1:3); that understanding and absorbing of the Spirit of God which renews "the spirit of the mind" and enables the believer to share the very thoughts of God, and so His Spirit.

### "The earnest of the Spirit"

The passages just considered are a help to our understanding of another saying of Paul:

> "God ... sealed us, and gave us **the earnest of the Spirit** in our hearts." (2 Corinthians 1:22, R.V.)

Once again we need to go back a little to follow Paul's reasoning. The "promises of God in Christ" are not matters of doubt, but are certain (verse 20):

> "Now he which establisheth us with you **in Christ**, and hath anointed us, is God ... " (verse 21)

Remarkably Paul has not written his more common "in Christ" (en Christō) here, but "into Christ" (eis Christon). Now this preposition eis is the opposite of the one we have already considered (ek, out of). Going "into Christ", we partake of him, that is of his spiritual mind and will. This is "the earnest of the Spirit", the pledge of the life of the Spirit, granted to the saints in the day of their flesh, as a guarantee of their fuller inheritance of the Spirit in the Kingdom to come. Because this essential understanding of the mind of the Spirit comes from God (through His words of truth, and belief and obedience), Paul can say they are "anointed" of God and are "sealed" of God. They have the Father's spiritual mark upon them, showing that they are His people (see also comment on Ephesians 1:13, pages 63-65).

### "The eternal Spirit"

> "If the blood of bulls and of goats ... sanctifieth to the purifying of the flesh: how much more shall the blood of Christ, who **through (the) eternal Spirit** offered himself without spot to God, purge your conscience from dead works to serve the living God?" (Hebrews 9:13-14)

103

What is this "eternal Spirit" through which Christ offered himself? The first impression would probably be that it is the power of the Holy Spirit. Perhaps with some surprise we discover that the article is missing: it is "through eternal Spirit", or "through an eternal spirit". The comments of some theological scholars make interesting reading. Swete (in his *The Holy Spirit in the New Testament*, page 252) translates "through an eternal spirit". Weymouth (*The New Testament in Modern Speech*) has a note: "lit. 'an eternal spirit', perhaps his own spirit". Ellicott's *New Testament Commentary* translates "through an eternal spirit" and has a remarkable note to the effect that this cannot be "the Holy Spirit" in the traditional sense.

What is this "Spirit", and why is it called "eternal"? A few New Testament parallels are helpful:

> *"Christ . . . born of the seed of David according to (the) flesh (kata sarka) . . . declared to be the Son of God with power, according to (the) spirit of holiness, by the resurrection of the dead . . ."*
>
> (Romans 1:4, R.V.)

Here the contrast is between "flesh" and "*a* spirit of holiness". Because Christ did not manifest the spirit of flesh, but rather a spirit, or mind, which was holy like that of his Father, God was able righteously to raise him from the dead. Clearly it was the spiritual mind of Christ—"not my will, but thine be done"—which made him acceptable to God.

There are interesting parallels in two other passages:

> *". . . great is the mystery of godliness; he who was manifest in (the) flesh, justified in (the) Spirit . . ."*  (1 Timothy 3:16, R.V.)

The "mystery of godliness" is that "secret" which was once concealed, but has now been revealed: the manifestation of God in human flesh, in the person of His Son. As Paul prays for the Colossians, that they may "know the mystery of God, even Christ, in whom are all the treasures of wisdom and knowledge hidden" (2:2-3, R.V.). Now in this manifestation Christ was "in flesh", but he was justified "in spirit" *(en sarki . . . en pneumati)*. These are the two terms used by Paul in Romans 8 to describe two categories. Those who are "in spirit" have a God-spirit and a Christ-spirit in their minds, because they have "set their minds on" spiritual things (see page 50 and Chapter 6). So Christ was justified (or accounted righteous, as the term means) "in spirit". This is not a reference to the Spirit nature he inherited after resurrection, for his "justification" had to occur *before* the resurrection, otherwise he would never have been raised to life at all! It is a reference to the "mind of the Spirit" which he shared with his Father.

> *"Christ suffered for sins ... being put to death in (the) flesh, but quickened in (the) spirit (sarki ... pneumati, as to flesh ... as to spirit)."*                                                                      (1 Peter 3:18)

Christ's flesh was literally "put to death" on the cross; but he had before that "put away" the mind of the flesh, in order that he might be "quickened in spirit". The same, says Peter, is true of the saints:

> *"Unto this end was the gospel preached even to the dead* (the spiritually dead in trespasses in sins, Ephesians 2:1) *that they might be judged according to men in (the) flesh (sarki,* as regards their flesh), *but live according to God in (the) spirit (pneumati,* as regards their spirit)"*
>                                                                               (1 Peter 4:6, R.V.)

These passages throw light on the meaning of the "eternal spirit" in which Christ offered himself. The same thought must be the explanation of another saying in Hebrews, that Christ has been made a priest for ever "after (the) power of an endless (or indissoluble) life" (7:16): not a reference to his immortality, but to the "eternal life" which he manifested in mind first in the days of his flesh, and which was prolonged into eternity after his resurrection.

The importance for us of the passages we have just been considering is great. Christ is seen to be our complete representative. He experienced the desires of his own nature ("in flesh"), but he put them aside to express the mind of God ("in spirit"). We too must strive to be "in spirit" in the same sense. It is in this way that we become sons and daughters of God, and heirs of the Kingdom.

### The Intercession of the Spirit

> *"In like manner the Spirit also helpeth our infirmity: for we know not how to pray as we ought: but the Spirit himself (itself, A.V.) maketh intercession for us with groanings which cannot be uttered; and he that searcheth the hearts knoweth what is the mind of the Spirit, because he maketh intercession for the saints according to the will of God."*
>                                                                            (Romans 8:26-27, R.V.)

This passage has always been found difficult to understand. Some have understood "the Spirit" here to refer to the spiritual mind of the believer; others to Christ or to the Spirit of God. The key expression is "makes intercession". Here are the passages where this thought occurs:

> *"Christ ... maketh intercession for us ..."*  (Romans 8:34)

> *"(Christ) ever liveth to make intercession for (those that draw near to God through him) ..."*  (Hebrews 7:25)

> *"Christ entered ... into heaven itself, now to appear in the presence of God for us ..."*  (Hebrews 9:24)

> *"... one mediator between God and men ... Christ Jesus."*  (1 Timothy 2:5)

How can the Spirit make intercession apart from Christ? Are there two intercessors? Paul must be referring to the intercession of Christ ("the Spirit") on our behalf, hence "the Spirit *himself*". Another difficulty is the expression "with groanings that cannot be uttered", often interpreted as "inarticulate longings" in the minds of the saints. Alfred Nicholls has a most helpful passage in *The Spirit of God*, pages 107-8, which all readers are recommended to study. The Greek implies not so much that the "groanings" are inarticulate as that they cannot "be known or repeated by us". The communion is between Christ and God on behalf of the saints.

### "Lydia ... whose heart the Lord opened"

> *"Lydia ... one that worshipped God, heard us: whose heart the Lord opened, to give heed unto the things spoken by Paul."*  (Acts 16:14)

*How* did God open Lydia's mind, or understanding? We are not told. We tend to read the narrative as if there were two consecutive actions: God opened Lydia's heart; then she gave heed, etc. But that is not at all certain. She was already a worshipper of God, no doubt having quite a knowledge of the law and the prophets. It is quite possible she had already heard something of this "gospel" being preached by Paul. Had a questioning already arisen in her mind, and was the hearing of the word of Paul the means by which God "opened her heart"? The nearest parallel is in Luke, where the same verb is used:

> *"Was not our heart burning within us ... while he opened to us the scriptures? ... Then opened (Jesus) their mind (understanding, A.V.) that they might understand the scriptures"*  (Luke 24:32,45, R.V.)

*"The entrance (opening, R.V.) of thy words giveth light."*

(Psalm 119:130)

This is certainly the Scriptural method. We may feel confident that it was so in Lydia's case.

## Conclusion

There is one important conclusion to be drawn from our survey of numerous Scriptural passages: there is grave risk of error in reading "the Spirit" or "the Holy Spirit" in a sense which we have already determined in our own minds. There are passages where the reference is to gifts of power, granted to servants of God in apostolic times, to enable them to witness effectively in their preaching; there are others where it is to the manifestation of the Spirit of God, in the "spiritual wisdom and understanding" which can be theirs through the Word of truth and grace. Only a careful comparison of Scripture with Scripture can reveal to us the truth on this vital subject. And when we have done all our studying, we shall realise that our salvation depends not upon some independent influence, descending upon us direct from God, but upon our understanding of and obedience to His truth through our humble submission to the message and the Spirit of His Word.

# 9

## THE ABIDING

WE turn finally to the passages of the New Testament which speak of that which "abides" or "dwells" in the faithful. In this area especially there is a temptation to emphasise certain phrases and to build a doctrine upon them, as for instance Paul's "Christ may dwell in your hearts" (Ephesians 3:17). When the relevant passages are collected, however, it becomes obvious at once that the apostles had a profound grasp of the truth of the matter, but that they express their understanding in a variety of ways. For example, the following are said to dwell or abide in the saints:

God and Christ; the Word, and words, of God and of Christ; what they had heard from the beginning; the truth; love; God's seed; eternal life. And prime conditions for this abiding are that the faithful "abide in the teaching of Christ" and "keep the commandments" of God and of Christ. (It is to be noted also that the great majority of these sayings are found in the writings of the Apostle John).

Now these inspired sayings must all be carefully examined, each one in its context, and then taken together. In this way we may hope to arrive at a full understandidng of all that was in the mind of the apostles.

### The Word, or Words

First, here is a list of passages where it is *the Word* or *words* of God and of Christ which are said to *abide* in the faithful:

*"Ye (Jews) have not **God's word** abiding in you"* (clearly implying that they ought to have had it).        (John 5:38)

*"Ye are clean* (verse 2, *cleansed*) *because of the **word** which I have spoken unto you. Abide in me and **I in you** ... He that abideth in me, and **I in him**, the same beareth much fruit* (that is, of the

Spirit, and not the works of the flesh) . . . *If ye abide in me, and* **my words** *(rhēmata: utterances, sayings, pronouncements) abide in you . . . If ye keep my commandments, ye shall abide in my love.''* (John 15:3-10, R.V.)

*"Young men . . . ye are strong, and the* **word of God abideth** *in you."* (1 John 2:14)

*"If that which* **ye heard** *from the beginning (the gospel)* **abide** *in you, ye also shall abide in the Son, and in the Father."* (1 John 2:24, R.V.)

*"The elder unto the elect lady and her children, whom I love in truth: and not I only, but also all they that* **know the truth***; for the* **truth***'s sake which* **abideth** *in us."* (2 John 1,2, R.V.)

What emerges from these passages is that *truth* is conveyed by the *Word* of God and of Christ. The Jews could not understand what Christ was saying, because they could not "hear his word" (John 8:43). They were natural, not spiritual, in outlook, and so "the word of God did not abide" in them. As devout Jews they no doubt knew the *text* of the Word of God well enough, but they had shut their minds to its spiritual import, because that would have demanded a reformation of their lives. They had not allowed it to "cleanse" them and as a result were "blind" and "dead". The point remains just as vital for us, so many centuries later.

It is interesting to note that when Jesus said, "If ye abide in me, and my *words* abide in you . . . ", he used the term *rhēma*, which means primarily an utterance, and then the principle of truth, a teaching. Remarkably he used the same term in this well known passage:

*"It is the spirit that quickeneth; the flesh profiteth nothing: the words (rhēmata) that I have spoken unto you, are spirit, and are life."* (John 6:63, R.V.)

The spirit and the life were not to consist of some mystical conception, called "word" or "spirit"; they were to arise from an understanding and heart-felt acceptance of the very sayings of the Lord. It is worth reminding ourselves once again that these "sayings of the Lord" are found in the written Word of God, and nowhere else.

In the apostle Paul's saying, it is to be noted that the effect of "the word of Christ" dwelling richly in a believer is an increase of spiritual wisdom. Now wisdom is sound judgement, based on knowing and understanding. What "dwells" in the believer is not mystical experience, but an attitude and disposition of mind resulting from this, called "the mind of Christ" by the same apostle in 1 Corinthians 2:16.

In John's phrase, "the truth" abides in the saints. But the truth has to be "known"—that is, it must first be understood, then appreciated, and then acted upon. Hence "thy children *walk in truth*" and "walk after his commandments" (2 John 4,6). "Knowing" the truth involves all these aspects.

## God Abiding in Us

A second condition for "the abiding" is laid down in John's Epistles:

> "*Whosoever shall confess that Jesus is the Son of God, God* **abideth in him**, *and he in God.*" (1 John 4:15, R.V.)

> "*Whosoever denieth the Son, the same hath not the Father: he that confesseth the Son* **hath the Father** *also.*" (1 John 2:23, R.V.)

Evidently to "have the Father" is the same thing as to have "God abiding in us".

Why does John make such a point of "confessing that Jesus is the Son of God"? The reason is made clearer by his assertions:

> Those "*who confess not that Jesus Christ is come in the flesh*" are deceivers. "*Whosoever goeth onward* (R.V.) *and abideth not in the doctrine of Christ, hath not God (abiding in him).*" (2 John 7,9)

These statements make it clear that John was referring to false ideas about the nature of Christ which were influencing some in his day. Those holding these ideas are generally labelled "gnostics" (from *gnōsis*, knowledge). They had "gone onward", beyond the clear teaching of Scripture, and were claiming a special knowledge. Among their teachings were the ideas that matter was inherently evil; only "the spirit" could commune with God. The believer could give himself to any physical activity in the quest of greater spiritual experience; this led to sexual excesses in the name of religion which explain the charges of "lasciviousness" made by Peter and Jude. Further, it was alleged, it was incredible that God would have manifested His Son in evil flesh; the real Son of God was not Jesus of Nazareth, but an 'emanation' from the Father called the Christ (anointed), which dwelt upon Jesus of Nazareth for his ministry but departed from him before his death on the cross. What died there was the man Jesus, not the Christ, the Son of God.

It is easy to see how such ideas, and indeed their modern counterpart in the doctrine of the trinity and the 'incarnate Son' (instead of the 'incarnate Father', that is, *God* manifested in flesh) were destroying the Scriptural doctrine of the atonement. The real Son of God, according to gnostic ideas, did not fully experience the temptations of mortal existence and therefore could not conquer the impulses to sin within his own flesh. "The devil" was therefore not destroyed in him (Hebrews 2:14), because there was no real "sacrifice of himself" (Hebrews 9:26); in other words, no real atonement for sin.

What emerges is the very important point that God cannot "abide in us" and we cannot "have the Father and the Son" unless we have a proper Scriptural understanding of the atonement. We need to know and to acknowledge the truth about human nature and its inherent rebelliousness against the will of God; then, the experience of Christ in overcoming this rebelliousness in himself and setting himself resolutely to do, not his own will, but the Father's, all of his own voluntary choice: "Lo I come to do thy will, O God"; then, his voluntary offering of himself as "the lamb of God that taketh away the sin of the world", the atonement for sin. By this supreme work in Christ, God was able in righteousness and in mercy to offer forgiveness of sins to all those who, receiving His Word and His promises in faith, would recognise these truths and humble themselves before Him in repentance. They would, in other words, have come to a Scriptural understanding of "the flesh" and "the spirit", and of the different minds which these influences produce, and so be able to reflect in themselves "the Spirit of God". In this way God could "abide in them" and they could "have the Father and the Son".

The example just considered illustrates once again the way in which expressions of spiritual truth depend for their proper understanding upon basic Scriptural teachings. The apostle John was striving to increase the "spiritual wisdom and understanding" of his readers; but he was presenting this, not as though it were a new and independent revelation, but as the fruit of the teachings which they had "heard from the beginning".

## Love

In two passages the apostle John asserts the prime importance of "love" as a condition of the "abiding".

> *"If we love one another,* **God abideth** *in us."*
>
> (1 John 4:12, R.V.)
>
> *"God is love; he that abideth in love abideth in God, and* **God abideth** *in him."* (verse 16, R.V.)

This introduces what has become an urgent and critical subject in recent times. The concept of "love" is now so perverted in popular usage and so emotionalised in modern religious use that the reader of the New Testament is in grave danger of being misled. These perversions of its true sense make it difficult to use the term "love" in writing or speaking without some clear explanation of what is meant.

The attitude of "love" is popularly interpreted as implying kindness and sympathy towards all, and as expressing itself in active work for the disadvantaged in society—the poor, the homeless, the disabled, for example. Since social service has largely become the modern, popular religion, such activities are seen by many as a proof of being genuinely 'Christian'.

Let it be said at the outset that we all have an obligation to help those in real need. But two considerations should be borne in mind: first, it is quite obvious that many who enthusiastically join in these activities have no religion of any kind—they are humanists or atheists; and second, it is important for us to ask what the *real* need is—is it present physical relief, or the need to be delivered from the ever present evil of sin and death? True, it may be necessary to help with the physical in order that the spiritual may be heard. But deliverance from sin and death is the main need; it should not be pushed into the background.

When, then, the true believers in God are urged to show "love", what is its nature? As is so often the case, the Old Testament gives us the key to the understanding of the New. Faithful

112

Israelites were commanded to treat with compassionate mercy the poor, the widows, the fatherless and the foreigners among them; they were to treat with special consideration the blind and the deaf; and not only, "Thou shalt not hate thy brother in thine heart", but "thou shalt love thy neighbour as thyself" (Leviticus 19). God's own explanation for these commands is set out thus:

*"Thou shalt remember that thou wast a bondman (slave) in Egypt, and the **LORD** thy God redeemed thee thence: therefore I command thee to do this thing."*     (Deuteronomy 24:18)

The principle is clear and effective: in His great mercy God had redeemed His people from slavery in Egypt, from which they could not have delivered themselves. They were therefore to show a like mercy to those of their fellows who were in need. So their attitude to their fellow Israelites was not to be based just on kindly feelings, or on good nature; it was to arise from a recognition of the great grace they had received and the obligation it placed upon them to act in the same spirit to others. So the "love" of the devout Israelite was not humanist; it was religious—it arose from a recognition of his own state of need. When in later centuries rulers in Israel cast aside this obligation, it was a clear sign that they had forgotten, or rejected, their own need of redemption.

The basis of the attitude of the followers of Christ is just the same:

*"Let all bitterness ... wrath ... anger ... clamour ... railing be put away from you, with all malice: and be ye kind one to another, tenderhearted, forgiving each other, **even as God also in Christ forgave you**. Be ye therefore **imitators of God** as beloved children; and walk in love, even as **Christ also loved you**, and gave himself up for us."*     (Ephesians 4:31—5:2, R.V.)

*"Herein is love, not that we loved God, but that **he loved us**, and sent his Son to be the propitiation for our sins. Beloved, if God so loved us, we ought also to love one another."*  (1 John 4:10-11)

And so, as the apostle Paul so aptly put it, "The love of Christ *constraineth* us" (2 Corinthians 5:14).

So John's, "If we love one another, *God abideth* in us" is explained. The believers are called upon to feel 'the constraint' of the love which God and Christ have shown to them, by manifesting the same mind towards one another as the Lord has shown towards them. In this way they are "begotten" of God; they are His "sons and daughters", because His spiritual mind is reproduced in them. In John's phrase "God abides" in them.

Once again, a vital Scriptural term, "love", is shown to have a doctrinal basis. Certain items of God's revelation have to be understood before the spiritual quality can be truly manifest. To claim to manifest this spirit of love without acknowledging the part that God and Christ have played, is humanism, which is one form of idolatry. Once again, too, the manifestation of God in the saints consists of the reflection in them of His Spirit, that is His mind and outlook. In this way He "abides" in them.

### "God's Seed"

*"Whosoever is begotten of God doeth no sin, because **his (God's)** seed abideth in him: and he cannot sin, because he is begotten of God."* (1 John 3:9, R.V.)

John does not mean that the sincere believer is bound to live a sinless life, but that he commits his life not to the indulgence of his own desire, but to the will of God; and God, who "knoweth our frame" and "remembereth that we are dust" (Psalm 103:14) will forgive the lapses of those who sincerely repent, and restore them to fellowship with Himself.

What then is "God's seed" which abides in the faithful? It arises from the fact that they are "begotten of God":

*"Having been begotten again, not of corruptible **seed**, but of **incorruptible, through the word of God** ... This is the word of good tidings which was preached unto you."* (1 Peter 1:23,25, R.V.)

*"Of his own will (God) begat us **with the word of truth**."* (James 1:18)

*"Except a man be born of water and **of spirit** ..."* (John 3:5)

*"It is the spirit that **quickeneth**; the flesh profiteth nothing; the words that I have spoken unto you are spirit and are life."* (John 6:63, R.V.)

The Word of God conveys the Spirit of His mind; when the believer receives and accepts it, he has a new understanding, a new mind. A new spiritual creature is begotten by God's incorruptible seed. He is a son (or daughter) of God, manifesting in mind and outlook the same spiritual quality as the Father. But if a man goes on living according to the desires of his flesh, he has in him not "God's seed", but "the seed of the serpent".

## "Eternal life"

*"Whosoever hateth his brother is a murderer: and ye know that no murderer hath eternal life abiding in him."*

(1 John 3:15)

The clear implication of John's saying is that if a man is *not* a murderer, but is one who loves his brother (upon the basis explained in the section on "Love" above), then he *has* "eternal life abiding in him".

What is meant by "eternal life" here? The subject has caused strife in the past, largely due to fears that important principles of Scripture truth were being denied, or false views asserted. The "present possession of eternal life" has been identified by some with a belief in "the present possession of the Holy Spirit", implying some power of God acting directly upon the heart and mind, weakening the need for reliance upon the Word of God, and giving the recipient a superior experience and an authority in determining truth.

There is only one sound way to answer our question: we must take a sober look at other passages which treat this theme. To begin with, some sayings of Jesus:

*"He that heareth my word, and believeth him that sent me, hath eternal life ... (he) hath passed out of death into life."*

(John 5:24, R.V.)

*"He that eateth my flesh and drinketh my blood hath eternal life; and I will raise him up at the last day."* (John 6:54, R.V.)

And then from the apostle John:

*"We know that we have passed out of death into life, because we love the brethren."* (1 John 3:14, R.V.)

*"God gave unto us eternal life, and this life is in his Son."*

(5:11, R.V.)

*"These things have I written unto you, that ye may know that ye have eternal life ..."* (verse 13, R.V.)

*"We know* (as a fact) *that the Son of God is come, and hath given us* **an understanding,** *that we may* **know** (intimately, by spiritual comprehension) *him . . . and we are* **in him** *that is true, even in his Son Jesus Christ. This is the true God, and* **eternal life."**

(verse 20)

The most helpful way to understand what is meant is to seek Scriptural parallels to the remarkable declaration of Jesus and John that the true believer has "passed out of death into life". Here are some:

(Jesus to Paul concerning his mission to the Gentiles):
*". . . to open their eyes, and to turn them from* **darkness** *to* **light,** *and from* **the power of Satan unto God,** *that they may receive forgiveness of sins."*

(Acts 26:18)

*"Ye were once* **darkness,** *but are now* **light in the Lord."**

(Ephesians 5:8, R.V.)

*"(God) hath delivered us from the* **power of darkness** *and hath* **translated** *us into the* **kingdom** *of his dear Son."*

(Colossians 1:13)

*"(God) called you out of* **darkness** *into his* **marvellous light."**

(1 Peter 2:9)

The basic key to the understanding of these sayings is found in the reply of Jesus to the man who wanted to go home and "bury his father" (that is, go home until his father died so that he would be able to receive his share of the family inheritance) before following the Lord: "Follow me . . . leave *the dead* to bury their own dead" (Matthew 8:22). Men and women are "dead in trespasses and sins", unless they are "quickened" (made alive) through the mercy of God (Ephesians 2:1). The ignorant Gentiles are "alienated from *the life of God* through the ignorance that is in them" (Ephesians 4:18), where the reference is clearly not immortality in the Kingdom, but to the state of being "quickened" through the revelation of God.

The above quotations teach us that in the sight of God the human being is in one of two states: either he is in the power of darkness, in the power of Satan, and is dead; or he has been delivered from that state and has been "quickened", transferred into the spiritual kingdom of Christ, and is "light in the Lord". He has been "born again", not of flesh but of spirit, and is

116

a "new creature", a "new man" in Christ. He is committed to living a new kind of life—not according to the natural desires of his flesh, but according to the will of God.

This is John's "eternal life", the mind of the Spirit, begotten and nourished through the Word of God. It is called "eternal" because it springs from the "eternal God" and is the result of His "eternal redemption" in Christ (Romans 16:26; Hebrews 9:12). The "eternal life" which abides in the saints arises from "understanding and knowing God and his Son" (John 17:3; 1 John 5:20) and is entirely consistent with the other expressions used in the New Testament for the same thought.

## Dwelling "in Christ" and "in God"

We come finally to a group of passages of special significance:

*"He that eateth my flesh and drinketh my blood **abideth in me**, and I in him . . ."* (John 6:56, R.V.)

*"**Abide in me**, and I in you . . . If ye abide in me, and my words (rhēmata, sayings, teachings) abide in you . . ."* (John 15:4,7)

*"He that keepeth his (Christ's) commandments **abideth in him**, and he in him."* (1 John 3:24, R.V.)

*"If we love one another, God abideth in us . . . Hereby know we that **we abide in him**, and he in us, because he hath given us of (ek) his Spirit."* (4:13, R.V.)

*"God is love; and he that abideth in love **abideth in God**, and God abideth in him."* (verse 16, R.V.)

These passages have all been quoted already; but we must now point out a remarkable feature of their teaching: for they all assert that not only do God and Christ dwell (or abide, R.V.) in the faithful, but that the faithful themselves *dwell in Christ and even in God.*

Now this aspect of the subject seems to be neglected by some who contend for the personal and independent dwelling of Christ in the saints. For if Christ dwells in us in an individual and personal way, what are we to say of *our* dwelling in Christ, and especially *in God*? Is that also personal and independent?

To put the matter thus is to make clear the truth. Our dwelling in Christ and in God must be of the same kind as their dwelling in us. That we could be "in God" in any physical or personal sense is impossible; but in a spiritual sense, in our understanding of the spiritual quality of God and of Christ, in the giving of our hearts and minds to it, and in our faithful service, there can be developed that "fellowship (common sharing) with the Father and the Son" (1 John 1:3), that "unity of the Spirit" (Ephesians 4:3) which makes us true sons and daughters of God. The "oneness" which was to exist between God, Christ and his servants would come about, said Jesus in his prayer for them in John 17, because "the words which thou (God) gavest me I have given unto them; and they received them and know of a truth that I came forth from thee ..." As a result "they have kept thy word", that word which is "truth" and was the means of sanctifying them. We have been privileged to be among those who have believed "through their word" and so to share their fellowship with the Father and the Son.

# 10

# CONCLUSIONS

ONE of the most important principles which emerge from the record of God's early dealings with Israel is that He used His almighty power to achieve not merely a physical, but even more a moral and spiritual end. Israel were delivered from the bondage of the Egyptians by the Spirit of God acting in power; but the purpose was not just the release of a people and their settlement in a new land; it was to impress upon that people the character of their God and Redeemer, and to form them to be His people.

Looking back on the experience of the Exodus 40 years later, Moses reminds them that no people had ever seen such demonstrations of Divine power as they had. They had not only seen signs and wonders and "great terrors", but they had heard "the voice of God speaking out of the midst of the fire". All this, says Moses, was to convince you that your God, the God of Israel, is alone God: "there is none else beside him". But it was also *"that he might instruct thee ... and thou heardest his words ... "* (Deuteronomy 4:35,36).

Those "words" of God, amplified in the Law He gave to Israel, revealed to them His true character of holiness and mercy. It was a revelation of the Spirit—or mind—of God, and also of the kind of lives they should live in His service, in order that they might be "a peculiar treasure unto me ... a holy nation". Now such a spiritual education could not be achieved instantaneously. It was inevitably a process which would take time, and therefore the instruction *had to be maintained,* especially for the generations still to be born. The means by which this was to be done were not left to Moses to devise. From the beginning of the Exodus pilgrimage to the Holy Land, Moses was told to "write the words of this law". So there was founded in Israel that written record

119

of the purpose of God for His people, of His principles of truth and righteousness, of His will for them in His service, of His judgements upon sinners and of His promises for the faithful. That written record grew as the centuries passed, with the accounts of the historical books, the words of instruction in Psalms and Prophets, and later still by the Gospels and Epistles of the New Testament. It remained throughout the ages the basic authority for determining the will of God, for understanding His truth, for the ordering of the faithful servants' ways before Him, at times when there was no inspired messenger to speak for Him. The Word of God has remained to our day the means chosen by Him to "instruct them", to promote the work of His Spirit.

## The Appeal of the Word

Now a most important question arises at this point: *How* has God chosen to approach men and women through His Word of truth? What is the character of His message for them and His appeal to them?

The answer is clear: it is a consistent appeal to their understanding upon a reasonable basis. The faith God appeals for in His servants is not an irrational or purely emotional experience. It is based upon reasonable grounds. Israel were redeemed from Egypt; so they should hear the words of the One who redeemed them. Jesus was raised from the dead; so the people should heed the words of His apostles who had seen the risen Christ. Truths are explained in clearly intelligible terms. Assurances of grace and favour are given, promises are made and warnings of judgement are uttered. The whole is an appeal to the common human ability—God-given in the first place—of being able to *understand* what God wishes to say. It is not primarily an appeal to the emotions, though there will be an emotional response from those who appreciate the message.

The purpose of this approach is significant. The Lord God of heaven is treating His creatures as *persons*, capable not only of understanding the truth He wants to convey to them, but of *making decisions* affecting their lives and their future. Having given them the ability to choose, He expects them to use it by choosing His way in preference to their own:

*"See"*, says Moses to Israel, *"I have set before thee this day life and good ... death and evil ... therefore choose life ... "*
(Deuteronomy 30:15,19)

*"Come, let us reason together"*, says God to them: *"If ye be willing and obedient ... but if ye refuse and rebel ... "*
(Isaiah 1:18-20)

And likewise Jesus: *"Whosoever heareth these sayings of mine, and doeth them ... And everyone that ... doeth them not ... "*
(Matthew 7:24-26)

If God's servants persevere in their choice of obedience, they become characters, individual personalities, reflecting God's mind in their ways. It is those characters which He proposes to prolong in a new kind of life in the age of come. This has been the work of the Spirit of God through His Word of truth right down the ages.

### Human Pride

Objections have been raised to this view of the matter. It has been said that to regard the work of the Spirit of God through His Word of truth in this way is to rely too much upon the human mind. But this is to misunderstand the situation. The human mind would never have thought of the wonders of God's truth, of His holiness and His infinite mercy in the redemption of sinners. If it had been left to the powers of the human mind there would have been no salvation for anyone. But it has *not* been left so. Let Paul explain:

*"Eye hath not seen, nor ear heard, neither have entered into the heart of man, the things which God hath prepared for them that love him.* **But God hath revealed them unto us** *by his Spirit ... "*
(1 Corinthians 2:9-10)

So the great things which were beyond the invention of the human mind have been revealed to us. Are we to treat this revelation as something beyond our understanding? Of course not. God has not only given us minds capable of understanding Him when He explains His truth, but also a revelation of Him designed to be understood. The whole approach of God to mankind through His Word assumes that this is the case. This is not to say that there are not in Scripture itself heights and depths of truth which we shall not completely understand. But that is not the point.

What we *do* need to understand for our devoted service to God has been explained in intelligible terms. That is what is essential to our salvation.

Again it has been argued that to view the work of God's Spirit thus is to foster a spiritual pride in our ability to understand it. But anyone who feels any pride in the fact that he has come to a knowledge of the truth certainly has not fully appreciated the revelation of God about himself as a creature of human flesh. Of all the weaknesses that Scripture exposes, pride is one of the most abhorrent to God. A total humility before Him and His Word of truth is characteristic of its teaching, and is well expressed in God's assurance to Israel:

> *". . . to this man will I look, even to him that is poor* (that is, *humble) and of a contrite spirit, and trembleth at my word."*
>
> (Isaiah 66:2)

"What hast thou that thou didst not receive?" We may apply Paul's words to the Corinthians in a general sense to our own case. Our predominant reaction should be one of profound thankfulness that God has seen fit to bring His revelation to our attention—in whatever remarkable way that has been achieved—and has given us minds capable of understanding it, and so responding to Him.

### The Words of Comfort

But are there not numerous passages in both the Old and New Testaments which testify to the real help and comfort which God will grant to His faithful? There are indeed—too many by far to quote, but here are a few:

> Nothing in the world *"shall be able to separate us from the love of God, which is in Christ Jesus our Lord."* (Romans 8:39)
>
> *"Blessed be God . . . the Father of mercies, and the God of all comfort; who comforteth us in all our tribulation . . . "*
>
> (2 Corinthians 1:3)
>
> *"My God shall supply all your need . . . "* (Philippians 4:19)
>
> *"Let us therefore come boldly unto the throne of grace, that we may obtain mercy, and find grace to help in time of need."*
>
> (Hebrews 4:16)

*"The God of all grace, who called you unto his eternal glory in Christ, after that ye have suffered a little while, shall himself perfect, stablish, strengthen you."* (1 Peter 5:10, R.V.)

What are we to do with such passages? Why, heartily believe them, of course. They encourage us to have complete confidence that God will do for us all that He sees fit in our daily service, and for all its needs. But we run into difficulties if we try to analyse exactly how God will do this. The Scriptures do not give us this exact analysis, and we shall do well to follow their example. In a very interesting article on "The Spirit of God", L. G. Sargent wrote this:

> "It is when we attempt to define *how* God works in us that we get into difficulties. It is when, consciously or unconsciously, we picture 'spirit' as some sort of substance that can come upon us and fill us—very tenuous and intangible, no doubt, but something that can flow like a gas—it is then that we find ourselves in all sorts of theological complications. The fact is that God wills; He makes known His mind; He works His will. Let us accept the facts and leave the means."
>
> (*The Christadelphian*, 1964, page 295)

The attempt to analyse the modes of activity of the Spirit of God in our lives is a frequent cause of damaging dissension. But it has another consequence, equally damaging, for the faithful are having their minds directed to the wrong objective. They are being encouraged to think of the Spirit of God in the saints as a refined form of physical power. Now it has been the consistent theme of these pages that its true significance is in the expression of God Himself as a spiritual and moral Being. God's own description of Himself to Moses: "The LORD, a God full of compassion and gracious, slow to anger, and plenteous in mercy and truth; keeping mercy for thousands, forgiving iniquity and transgression and sin: and that will by no means clear the guilty . . ." (Exodus 34:6-7, R.V.)—here is the essential Spirit of the Lord in all His holiness, His mercy and His truth. It received its greatest manifestation in the "grace and truth" which dwelt in His only-begotten Son.

This is the Spirit which the servants of God are called upon to manifest themselves, in order that they might be "begotten of

God'', ''born of the Spirit'', ''sons and daughters of the living God''. To prepare them for this great rôle and to warn them against the natural spirit generated by their own ''fleshly lusts, which war against the soul'' (1 Peter 2:11), they have been granted the God-breathed Scriptures, deliberately designed for ''teaching, for reproof, for correction, for discipline (R.V. margin) in righteousness'', that as men and women of God they may be ''complete, furnished completely unto every good work'' (2 Timothy 3:16, R.V.). Through the spiritual power of the Word of God they can avoid being ''fashioned according to this world'' and instead be ''renewed in the spirit of their minds'' (Romans 12:2). By this means and by the gracious care of God through the Lord Jesus we shall be ''delivered from this present evil world''. This is the great opportunity and privilege which is being offered to us by the Spirit of God. Let us see that our attention is not diverted to matters of uncertain definition and secondary importance, for they will distract our minds from the main work of God in us, for in the end they are irrelevant to our salvation.

One final thought for our comfort. In our difficulties over understanding what God will or will not do for us by His Spirit, it may help us to think of the subject as having two complementary aspects: first, that of God in heaven, who looks down upon the children of men, and has set in motion the process by which we may be saved from sin and death, and who will certainly do everything needful in His wisdom for the good of His children; and second, ourselves upon the earth, whose greatest need is to commit ourselves to God in prayer, in total trust and confidence that He will do for us all that He sees necessary for our spiritual welfare; and then to maintain our commitment to that ''word of his grace'' which is able to build us up and to give us at last that inheritance among the sanctified.

May God grant us to direct our thoughts and our energies away from contentious issues which cannot be precisely decided, and towards the development of that ''spiritual wisdom and understanding'' which is the real fruit of the Spirit of God in us.

# APPENDIX

Below is a list of significant passages where the Greek text *omits* the definite article (the) before "Holy Spirit", "Spirit" or "spirit". In each case it is inserted in the A.V. (K.J.V.).

**Matthew**
1:18
1:20
3:11
22:43

**Mark**
1:8

**Luke**
1:15
1:35
1:41
1:67
3:16
4:1
11:13

**John**
1:33
3:5
7:39
20:22

**Acts**
1:2
1:5
2:4
4:8
4:31
6:3
6:5
7:55
8:15
8:17
8:19
9:17
10:38
11:16
11:24
13:9
13:52
19:2 (2)

**Romans**
2:29
5:5
8:1
8:4
8:5
8:9 (3)
8:13
8:14
8:15 (2)
9:1
14:17
15:13
15:16
15:19

**1 Corinthians**
2:4
2:13
12:3
14:2

**2 Corinthians**
3:6 (1st)
3:18
6:6

**Galatians**
3:3
4:29
5:5
5:16
5:18
5:25 (2)

**Ephesians**
2:22
3:5
5:18
6:18

**Philippians**
2:1
3:3

**Colossians**
1:8

**1 Thessalonians**
1:5
1:6

**2 Thessalonians**
2:13

**1 Timothy**
3:16

**2 Timothy**
1:14

**Titus**
3:5

**Hebrews**
2:4
6:4
9:14

**James**
2:26

**1 Peter**
1:2
1:12
1:22
4:6

**2 Peter**
1:21

**Jude**
v. 19
v. 20

**Revelation**
1:10
4:2
17:3
21:10

———————

**TOTAL: 94**

125

# INDEX OF
# PRINCIPAL PASSAGES DISCUSSED

## OLD TESTAMENT

| Scripture | Page No. | Scripture | Page No. |
|---|---|---|---|
| **EXODUS** | | **JOSHUA** | |
| 24:3-4 | 15 | 1:7-8 | 16 |
| 33:18-19 | 12 | **PSALMS** | |
| 34:6-7 | 12,71,123 | 19:7-11 | 17 |
| **NUMBERS** | | 119 (various) | 39 |
| 11:25 | 9 | **ISAIAH** | |
| **DEUTERONOMY** | | 11:2-4 | 13 |
| 4:32-34 | 5 | 63:7-9 | 11 |
| 4:36 | 8 | **HOSEA** | |
| 4:39 | 7 | 6:6 | 14 |
| 17:18-20 | 16 | **MICAH** | |
| 24:18 | 14,113 | 3:8 | 21 |
| 31:9-13 | 15 | | |

## NEW TESTAMENT

| Scripture | Page No. | Scripture | Page No. |
|---|---|---|---|
| **MATTHEW** | | **JOHN (continued)** | |
| 4:23-25 | 22 | 5:38 | 108 |
| 13:23 | 48 | 6:63 | 109,114 |
| **MARK** | | 8:23,42-44 | 87 |
| 16:20 | 29 | 14:16,26 | 28,92-95 |
| **LUKE** | | 14:20-23 | 94 |
| 1:15-17 | 20 | 15:3-10 | 108,109 |
| 9:1,2,6 | 25 | 15:26,27 | 28,92-95 |
| 9:52-56 | 25 | 16:7-14 | 28,92-95 |
| 10:1,9 | 25 | **ACTS** | |
| 10:17-20 | 26 | 1:5,8 | 28,64 |
| 11:13 | 101 | 2:1-4 | 28 |
| 24:48-49 | 28 | 2:36-38 | 99-101 |
| **JOHN** | | 5:12-16 | 29 |
| 1:13 | 49,87 | 8:6-8 | 30 |
| 3:5 | 114 | 9:31 | 32 |
| | | 10:47-48 | 31 |
| | | 16:14 | 106 |
| | | 19:2 | 52 |

| Scripture | Page No. |
| --- | --- |

**ROMANS**
1:4 ...................104
7:22-25.................73
8:2-9...................50
8:2-16 ...............54-58
8:26-27................105
14:17 ..................82
15:13 ..................82

**1 CORINTHIANS**
1:18,23-24 ..............60
2 (various) ...........61-63
6:16-19.................84
12:7-11.................33
14 (various) ..........34,35

**2 CORINTHIANS**
1:20-22 .............65,103
3:3,17,18 ...........84-86
4:6 ....................72
5:14 ..................113
6:4-7...................81

**GALATIANS**
3:2-5 ................96,97
3:14 .............95,96,98
3:27-29................98
4:6,19.................97
4:28,29................96
5:16-25 .............58,59

**EPHESIANS**
1:13-14.................63
1:17-18 ..............65,66
2:14-18 ..............66,67
2:20-22................69
3:16-21 .............70-76
4:1-3 ...............68,118
4:4-6...................69
4:11-13................76
4:31,32 ............75,113
5:17-20................70
6:10-17 .............78,79

**PHILIPPIANS**
2:1 ....................90
2:5-8...................76
4:6-7...................79

**COLOSSIANS**
1:9-11.................77

**1 THESSALONIANS**
4:3-8..................83

**2 THESSALONIANS**
2:13...............88,89

**1 TIMOTHY**
3:16 ..................104

**2 TIMOTHY**
3:15-17................37

**TITUS**
3:5-6..................91

**HEBREWS**
2:3-4..................33
9:13-14 ...........103,104
10:5-6.................24

**JAMES**
1:18...............49,114
3:14-18................47

**1 PETER**
1:2 ...................89
1:3-5..................79
1:22-25 ...........49,114
3:18 .................105
4:6 ..................105

**1 JOHN**
1:3 ..................118
2:14,24...............109
3:9 ..................114
3:15 .................115
3:24...............87,117
4:10-11...............113
4:12,16...............112
4:13...............87,117
4:15 .................110

**2 JOHN**
vv. 1,2...............109
vv. 7,9...............110